BADER
Reading and Language Inventory

Fifth Edition

Lois A. Bader
Michigan State University

PEARSON

Merrill
Prentice Hall

Upper Saddle River, New Jersey
Columbus, Ohio

Library of Congress Cataloging-in-Publication Data
Bader, Lois A.
   Bader reading and language inventory/Lois A. Bader.—5th ed.
      p.cm.
   Includes bibliographical references.
   ISBN 0-13-119617-0
      1. Reading—Ability testing. 2. Language arts—Ability testing. I. Title: Reading and
language inventory. II. Title.
LB1050.46.B33 2005
428'.0076—dc22   2004052429

Vice President and Executive Publisher: Jeffery W. Johnston
Senior Editor: Linda Ashe Montgomery
Editorial Assistant: Laura J. Weaver
Production Coordination: Jolynn Feller, Carlisle Publishers Services
Production Editor: Linda Hillis Bayma
Design Coordinator: Diane C. Lorenzo
Cover Designer: Thomas Borah
Cover image: Getty One
Production Manager: Pamela D. Bennett
Director of Marketing: Ann Castel Davis
Marketing Manager: Darcy Betts Prybella
Marketing Coordinator: Tyra Poole

This book was set in Times by Carlisle Communications, Ltd. It was printed and bound by Courier Kendallville,
Inc. The cover was printed by Coral Graphic Services, Inc.

The reader's passage "Waukewa's Eagle" is based on "Waukewa's Eagle" by James Buckham, published by
D. Appleton-Century Company, Inc. in *St. Nicholas Magazine,* © 1900 and 1928.

Earlier edition © 1983 by Lois Bader

Pearson Education Ltd.
Pearson Education Singapore Pte. Ltd.
Pearson Education Canada, Ltd.
Pearson Education—Japan

Pearson Education Australia Pty. Limited
Pearson Education North Asia Ltd.
Pearson Educación de Mexico, S.A. de C.V.
Pearson Education Malaysia Pte. Ltd.

10 9 8 7 6 5 4
ISBN: 0-13-119617-0

PREFACE

The fifth edition of the *BADER Reading and Language Inventory* has been carefully revised to improve its formatting and accessibility, provide carefully constructed questions to fit the experience of English Language Learners, offer additional case study examples, and provide more reliability information. The most significant revision has been to address the needs of English Language Learners.

ELL Coverage: Because this inventory houses many special resources for assessing English Language Learners, it has long been a favorite for educators who work with students whose first language is not English. Special attention has been paid to the comprehension questions given after each reader's passage. They have been carefully reviewed and revised to ensure they meet the needs of less experienced English language readers.

Videotape: New also to this edition is a tool for teacher educators, a videotape designed for coursework to illustrate how to initiate testing through the student interest surveys, how to use the graded word lists, and how to assess students' reading levels with the reader's passages in the test battery. Those who use this inventory can now observe how certain tests are administered to first graders, fourth graders, and sixth graders.

Case Excerpts: Areas identified by researchers as essential for reading growth—phonemics, phonics, vocabulary, comprehension, and fluency—can be assessed efficiently with this inventory, but subtests for other important abilities are included as well. Case excerpts have been added to illustrate patterns of behavior that indicate a need to refer learners for further evaluation in vision, hearing, learning disabilities, speech, and language.

Flowcharts: Although earlier editions of the inventory contained tests to assess phonemic awareness and emergent literacy, the subtests pertaining to these areas have been moved forward in a revised sequence, and more information is available about how and when to use them. Flowcharts, located on the inside front and back covers, explain the order for using each subtest. Flowcharts for quick screening, basic literacy assessment, and diagnostic testing are on the inside front cover, and the flowchart for preliteracy/emergent literacy can be found on the inside back cover.

ACKNOWLEDGMENTS

Through five editions, national leaders in reading have generously shared their expertise with careful, insightful manuscript reviews. For this edition I wish to thank Linda Clinard, University of California, Irvine; Kathleen Endaya, Director, Project READ Literacy Program, Redwood City, California; Betty Higgins, Sam Houston State University; Maria H. Koonce, Florida Atlantic University; Ula Manzo, California State University, Fullerton; Michael Seth Mott, Purdue University, Calumet; Dan Pearce, Texas A&M University, Corpus Christi; Sue Rogers, Averett College; Rachel Salas, University of North Carolina at Greensboro; and Ethel Young, Kean University. My appreciation is extended to Katherine Weisendanger, Alfred University, for her early contributions; Michelle Johnston, Ferris University, for the case study; and Linda Clinard, Director of the California Reading and Literature Project at the University of California, Irvine, for the use of the adult thematic word lists. I also wish to thank Scott Bader, who provided the drawings appearing in the *Reader's Passages and Graded Word Lists* that accompanies this inventory, and I would also like to acknowledge the assistance of Sarah Crockett for this edition.

I am most grateful to my editor, Linda Montgomery, for her wise guidance, enthusiasm, and support. Vice president and publisher Jeff Johnston provides leadership for a wonderful team, each striving for excellence: production editor Linda Bayma, managing editor JoEllen Gohr, manufacturing manager Pam Bennett, cover design coordinator Diane Lorenzo, and marketing manager Darcy Betts Prybella. Editorial assistant Laura Weaver is appreciated for her warmth and efficiency. Project editor Jolynn Feller, Carlisle Communications, was especially helpful.

CONTENTS

PART ONE

Using the BADER Reading and Language Inventory

BADER
READING AND LANGUAGE
INVENTORY

INTRODUCTION

The *BADER Reading and Language Inventory* was constructed for use by teachers of K–12 and adult students and by literacy specialists and resource teachers, including teachers of English language learners. The design of the inventory offers examiners the flexibility to obtain information for several purposes: to determine literacy levels, to plan instruction, and to make referrals to appropriate specialists. Additional reasons for administering the inventory include measuring a student's progress, assessing the effectiveness of specific reading approaches, and diagnosing specific literacy needs. Because students experiencing difficulty in learning to read may have problems in other areas, several informal tests are provided so that their needs and abilities can be assessed. Portions of the inventory can be used for quick screening or initial placement of students.

Individual tests have long been recommended by professional authorities for those students who fail group-administered tests. The inventory provides valid, reliable procedures for individual assessment, as well as subtests and checklists to discover inhibiting conditions that can be improved with appropriate instruction.

Teachers of children, adolescents, and adults have instructional decisions to make. They also make referrals to specialists in vision, hearing, and language development when appropriate. Yet, most teachers have teaching responsibilities that make individual, in-depth evaluation difficult. Reading and learning specialists have demands on their time, too. This inventory was developed to meet the needs of teachers and specialists for a diagnostic battery, efficient in administration and interpretation, that encompasses vital areas of evaluation based on research. To the extent that students' strengths and needs are understood, they can be helped to learn.

Assessment Model

A thorough assessment includes personal interviews and reflections, observations, informal and formal tests, and diagnostic teaching. Experienced teachers learn to look for patterns of behavior as they observe learner strengths and needs. The inventory provides several tools and guides for this model. However, the quest for pertinent information should be balanced against the need not to distress the student or take time from instruction by overtesting.

Content of the Inventory

Student Priorities and Interests: Several inventories and checklists are provided to assess the interests and priorities of children, teens, and adults. Interests and priorities of non-English-speaking learners should be obtained from their English-speaking contacts.

English Language Screening: The English Language Learning test can be used for initial screening. The test begins with a list of questions requiring either one-word or concrete replies. Upper-level items require longer replies and give information about student concerns. An English Language Learning (ELL) Checklist helps the instructor monitor development.

Word Recognition Lists: Word recognition lists include a graded word list, experiential word lists, and thematic lists. The graded word list is a series of 10 words at each level from preprimer (PP) through eighth grade, plus a list designated as high school. Researchers and numerous test users have reported the reading level estimate of the word list to be highly accurate so that it may be used alone for screening or initial placement. This test provides an estimate of the reader's level of literacy so the examiner can select an entry level to the graded paragraphs. In addition, the graded list can serve as a quick check of the student's word recognition and word analysis abilities. Finally, by contrasting the reader's ability to read words in context with word recognition in isolation, the examiner can obtain some information about the reader's ability to use context as an aid to word recognition.

Four experiential word lists are provided: Instructional Directions List, Experience List I, Experience List II, and Functional Literacy List. The first list contains 15 words frequently used in instructional materials and tests. The experience lists each contain 15 words that beginning readers may have learned in daily life. The functional list contains 15 words that may be encountered in completing forms and managing personal affairs in daily life.

Three adult thematic word lists provide vocabulary on basic and intermediate levels. The themes are health and safety, office, and vehicles.

Graded Reading Passages: The reading passages range from preprimer through twelfth-grade level in difficulty. The passages have been designed to enable the examiner to assess comprehension and word recognition abilities so that the reader's instructional level might be determined.

Three sets of passages have been constructed for each level. The content of the first set has been written or adapted from the kinds of materials used in readers in the primary levels and content-area materials in secondary levels; this set is designated C, for children. The second set has been designed for use with children, adolescents, or adults; it is designated C/A, for children and adults. The third set is intended for use with adults; it is designated A, for adults, but may also be used with adolescents. The PP to third-grade A passages are intended for adults at the beginning reading levels. On the intermediate levels, the adult passages have been designed to assess functional literacy in life-role areas. Beyond the eighth-grade level, all passages have been constructed to assess reading in areas such as history, science, and citizenship. There is a balance of narrative and expository passages.

Phonics and Structural Analysis: The phonics and structural analysis inventories contain 11 subtests to be given selectively to obtain information pertinent to areas of knowledge and abilities that may underlie word recognition. These tests include Single Consonants, Consonant Blends, Consonant Digraphs, Vowel Digraphs, Long Vowel Sounds, Short Vowel Sounds, Reversals, Inflectional Suffixes, Derivational Suffixes, Prefixes, and Compound Words.

Spelling Tests: Seven spelling tests are provided. These may be given selectively to obtain information about the student's abilities in auditory and visual discrimination and memory, cognitive language development, sound-symbol association, and knowledge of spelling conventions. Spelling analysis can serve as a quick assessment of phonics knowledge and application. Although the primary use of each test is suggested in the title, additional kinds of information may be obtained. These tests and their levels are:

1. Words with silent letters, P–2
2. Words with silent letters, 3+
3. Words spelled phonetically, P–2
4. Words spelled phonetically, 3+
5. Words illustrating common spelling conventions, 2–4
6. Words illustrating common spelling conventions, 5+
7. Words commonly misspelled

Visual and Auditory Discrimination: Visual and Auditory Discrimination tests are provided for screening and referral purposes. A comparison of the results of these tests with spelling, phonemic, and reading performance may reveal patterns of behavior that are useful in making referrals to specialists.

Preliteracy and Emerging Literacy: Tests are presented to assess the development of prereading skills. While information obtained from these tests is invaluable when testing emergent literacy, a comprehensive evaluation must include additional subtests from the Oral Language, Interest Inventory, and Spelling Tests subsections in addition to visual and auditory screening. The tests in this section include Literacy Concepts, Phonemic Awareness, Rhyme Recognition, Initial Phoneme Recognition, Blending, Segmenting, Letter Knowledge, Hearing Letter Names in Words, and Syntax/Word Matching. Older readers who have difficulty with beginning reading may benefit by assessing their abilities and knowledge in these areas.

Cloze Tests: Four cloze tests are included to be used selectively to assess knowledge and abilities in semantic, syntactic, and grammatical processing. These tests may be read either to the student or by the student. They are:

- Cloze tests for beginning readers
- Semantic closure
- Syntactic closure
- Grammatical closure

Evaluation of Language Abilities: Instructions for obtaining samples of reader performance in various language areas and checklists for evaluation are provided. Language areas include:

- Oral language expression
- Oral language reception
- Written language expression
- Handwriting

Open-Book Reading Assessment: Instructions for constructing open-book reading assessments are provided to enable teachers to learn more about students' abilities to read academic, workplace, or life-role materials.

Arithmetic: The Arithmetic test includes a brief test of ability in the areas of addition, subtraction, multiplication, fractions, division, and decimals. This test is particularly useful in screening older students and adults. A higher score in math than reading may be an indicator of possible reading potential.

ADMINISTERING THE INVENTORY

Preparation for Using the Inventory

Materials for administering the various parts of the inventory are contained in this book; the readers' passages and a second copy of the word lists are provided in a separate booklet for the student. Prepare for testing by duplicating score sheets, checklists, and either K–12 or adult summary sheets, and place them in files for ready access. Folders may be labeled as Interest Inventories, Word Lists, Passages, Spelling, and so on, with more specificity reflecting the population you test: primary, upper elementary, secondary, and adult learners. Before each testing, assemble a packet of sheets appropriate to the age and anticipated ability range of the student.

The interest inventories, word lists, and passages of the *BADER Reading and Language Inventory* provide an initial framework for assessment. Additional tests in the inventory may be given as needed. Time for giving the inventory usually depends on the number of passages the student must read before reaching a frustration level, as well as on the number of individual subtests given. In any one session, the total amount of time spent testing probably should not exceed 30 minutes for young children or 60 minutes for older students. The primary reason for terminating testing is that the student's level of fatigue or interest has been exceeded.

Collecting Student Background Information: Forms are included to assist in the collection of background information, if it is available from home or the classroom teacher. The adult intake information form includes the adult interview and referral information (see pp. 154–157).

Testing Sequences: Flowcharts

Start by giving an interest inventory to establish rapport, observe language facility, and determine reader interests. Next, administer the graded word lists to determine a starting point for the graded passages. Use the supplementary word lists, if appropriate. Administer the graded passages to ascertain the student's reading level.

After determining reading level, decide what additional information regarding the student's skills development and reading processing is necessary for diagnostic teaching. Specify what areas need to be assessed and then select appropriate subtests. Give the student enough individual tests to determine literacy needs, strengths, and patterns of performance.

The sequence for administering subtests depends on several factors, including the ability level of the reader, time allotment, and objectives for testing. Flowcharts with page numbers are provided inside the front and back covers for preliteracy, K–12, and adult literacy, and for quick screening and diagnostic testing. Although the charts are provided for the users' convenience, the actual selection and sequence of subtests depends on the individual student and situation.

Give the preliteracy tests to nonreaders and struggling beginning readers who are unable to score above the preprimer level on the graded word lists and passages. Select tests primarily from the preliteracy section. Assess metalinguistic skills by starting with either the language or the print awareness subcategories. The suggested order for administering these subcategories may be altered according to the individual testing situation. The sequence presented is only one of several valid options but may prove helpful to inexperienced teachers or specialists. Some nonreaders may be able to complete the easier subtests from Phonics and Word Analysis tests. They may have learned the alphabet and consonant letter–sound associations, for example, yet not be able to read.

Children in the upper grades and teens who are reading on or close to grade level, but struggling in school, should be given an open-book reading assessment (OBRA) on content-area material most frequently used in their classes. Adults reading on or above the fourth-grade level should be given an OBRA on daily life, workplace, or academic material if they are in school.

Getting Optimum Results from Testing

1. *Create a relaxed atmosphere.* This is easily established if testing is done by the classroom teacher in a familiar environment. Problems may arise if the student is placed in a strange situation and tested by an unknown person. Under these circumstances, try to ensure that the student is comfortable, as this might affect his or her performance and result in an inaccurate diagnosis. Be a good listener.
2. *Assess both acquired and deficient skills.* Learn about student interests. To improve a student's self-confidence, start with what the student knows. Based on your

assessment, an instructional program can be designed that focuses initially on strengths.

3. *Be efficient.* Diagnosis based on a limited quantity of data may result in the examiner drawing erroneous conclusions. The data must be extensive enough to get an accurate account of reading behaviors with challenging materials. However, overextending the diagnosis may prove stressful. Administering additional tests that do not supply useful information could be both unnecessary and counterproductive.

4. *Make statements about the student's reading that are based on the data obtained.* Be careful not to extend the information and supply reasons for the reading problem that may be inaccurate. Some examiners are too quick to blame poor home environment for reading difficulties when the problem results from other circumstances.

5. *Determine the coping strategies of students.* When students read orally from either word lists or context, record the specific miscues. This might give insight into the student's patterns of performance and assist in the selection of individual subtests.

6. *Include trial teaching when circumstances permit.* The learner's response not only provides more diagnostic information but the teacher or tutor who works with the learner also can be given useful strategies to plan instruction.

Note: This inventory is particularly helpful for finding the achievement level of students at extreme reading levels. Group-administered, standardized tests do not give information about performance at very low or very high levels. Those reading either below or above their grade-level placement should be individually assessed to determine appropriate placement in materials for instruction. This inventory is also useful for testing students who are reading at grade level but have specific skill needs such as spelling or writing.

SUMMARIZING THE ASSESSMENT DATA

The results of the student evaluation can be summarized on the *BADER Reading and Language Inventory* summary sheets (K–12 or adult; see pp. 147–157). The K–12 form contains the following categories: Reading Profile, including instructional level and needs in reading; Language Development Needs; Instructional Needs in Spelling, Handwriting, and Arithmetic; Visual and Auditory Difficulties; Emergent Literacy; Student Strengths, Priorities, Interests, and Concerns; and Recommendations for Instruction. The adult form contains information useful in tutoring for basic literacy and English language learners. Copies of relevant checklists or subtests of the inventory and other samples of the student's work can be stapled to the summary sheet to provide more specific information.

The examiner is encouraged to give as few or as many tests as seem to be appropriate. The examiner's recommendations for instruction should be made on all observations and information available, including the student's interests and attitudes as well as the instructional assistance that will be available. When possible, trial teaching should be done to verify diagnosis and the selection of appropriate methods. Therefore, this assessment de-emphasizes conclusions drawn from quantification of a few limited samples of behavior. Teachers, as well as reading and learning specialists, are encouraged to consider the student's abilities and needs from a holistic perspective.

PART TWO

Test Battery

STUDENT PRIORITIES AND INTERESTS

The priorities of the learner are paramount in planning instruction. Not only will learning be more rapid if the student is working in areas of interest and concern, but instructional sessions will also be more pleasant. In addition, students often know the nature of their reading needs and can provide useful diagnostic information.

Select portions of the Student Priorities and Reading Interests Checklists that seem appropriate. Explaining as necessary, read them to or with the student. Then reread each section and ask the student what is first in importance, then second, third, and fourth.

Student Priorities I Checklists I.1 and I.2 may be used with children or adults on reading levels 1–8. Use I.1 with nonreaders and beginning readers and I.2 with readers on grade levels 2–8. (Do not use both.) Lists I.3 and I.4 can be used to identify topics of interest for younger (I.3) and older (I.3 plus I.4) students. Follow up with discussion. For example, if a student selects a general category such as animals, ask which animals are of most interest and why.

Student Priorities II Checklists is recommended for use with secondary and college students. Ask students to check areas of concern and then go back over the list and prioritize. Be sure to include each student's top priorities in the instructional plan. The priorities and interests lists can be used with a group by showing a transparency of each page to students who have been provided with their own copies. Later, students can be grouped and regrouped on the basis of specific needs and interests.

Unfinished Sentences are of most value to get acquainted with younger students. Ask the child to finish each sentence. Demonstrate as necessary. If a response is not forthcoming on an item, just move on. Quickly jot down a word or two to help you remember the most significant responses so as to maintain spontaneity. After the task is completed, engage the child in a discussion of topics that will help you get better acquainted and establish rapport.

STUDENT PRIORITIES I

I.1 I need specific help with: (OR)

A. _____ Letters of the alphabet

B. _____ Sounds for letters of the alphabet

C. _____ Meanings of words

D. _____ Remembering what I hear

E. _____ Understanding what I hear

F. _____ Writing my name

G. _____ Reading street signs

H. _____ Using the telephone book

I. _____ Reading directions

J. _____ Reading words on food packages

K. _____ Reading menus

L. _____ Reading the *TV Guide*

M. _____ Reading related to work

N. _____ Other (please specify): _____

I.2 I need specific help with:

A. _____ Short words

B. _____ Long words

C. _____ Sounds of each letter

D. _____ Sounds of letters together

E. _____ Reading faster

F. _____ Meanings of words

G. _____ Understanding what I read

H. _____ Remembering what I read

I. _____ Remembering what I hear

J. _____ Writing notes or letters

K. _____ Spelling

L. _____ Handwriting

M. _____ How to study

N. _____ Other (please specify): _____

STUDENT READING INTERESTS

I.3 I would like to be helped to read about:

_____ Adventures

_____ Mysteries

_____ Sports

_____ Comics

_____ Humor

_____ TV and movie stars

_____ Animals

_____ Nature

_____ Science

_____ History

_____ Other: _____

I.4 (Continue with older students)

_____ Careers

_____ Want ads

_____ Personal problems

_____ Travel

_____ Romance

_____ Home repair

_____ Children's books

_____ Religions/spiritual

_____ Gardening

_____ Cooking

_____ Crafts

_____ Mechanics

_____ Carpentry

_____ Sewing/needlework

_____ Other: _____

Student Priorities and Interests

STUDENT PRIORITIES II

II.1 I need specific help with this area (✓) or I have a strength in this area (+):

A. _____ Long words

B. _____ Short sentences

C. _____ Long sentences

D. _____ Punctuation

E. _____ Reading faster

F. _____ Meanings of words

G. _____ Understanding what I read in:

_____ Paragraphs

_____ Short selections (short stories, essays, etc.)

H. _____ Remembering what I read

I. _____ Remembering what I hear

J. _____ Picking out what to remember when I read

K. _____ Paying attention while I'm reading

L. _____ Telling about what I've read

M. _____ Criticizing what I've read

N. _____ Spelling

O. _____ Handwriting

P. _____ Knowing what to say when I'm writing

Q. _____ Knowing how to organize ideas when writing

R. _____ Knowing how to write correctly

S. _____ Writing research papers

T. _____ Taking tests

U. _____ Using the library

V. _____ Doing computer searches

II.2 I want to study material connected with:

A. The courses I am taking in: _____

_____ .

B. My job as a (manual, directories, direction): _____

_____ .

C. My practical needs such as (forms, maps, schedules): _____

_____ .

D. My hobby: _____

_____ .

II.3 I like to read about: _____

_____

_____ .

A. I would like to read about: _____

_____ .

B. I would like to read:

_____ Newspapers   Parts _____

_____ Magazines   Kinds _____

_____ Short stories   Types _____

_____ Fiction   Types _____

_____ Nonfiction   Topics _____

_____ Comics   Kinds _____

_____ Other _____

C. My strengths in reading, writing, and learning are: _____

_____ .

II.4 I prefer to work

_____ In a small group with a tutor

_____ With another student

_____ Individually with a tutor

UNFINISHED SENTENCES

1. Sometimes I like to _____ .

2. Last summer I _____ .

3. I hope I'll never _____ .

4. When I read I _____ .

5. My friend likes to _____ .

6. I often worry about _____ .

7. The best thing about school is _____ .

8. Someday I want to _____ .

9. The person I like best is _____ .

10. I wish someone would _____ .

11. Learning to read is _____ .

12. My favorite television show is _____ .

13. The worst thing about school is _____ .

14. I have fun when _____ .

15. The biggest problem with reading is _____ .

16. After school I like to _____ .

17. I wish my teacher would _____ .

18. My eyes are _____ .

19. I would like to be able to read _____ .

20. If I had three wishes I would wish for _____

_____

_____ .

Notes from follow-up discussion: _____

_____

_____ .

ENGLISH LANGUAGE LEARNING

The English Language Learning (ELL) Quick Start test can be used for initial screening or progress testing when there is no time or resources for in-depth evaluation. Schools, agencies, and community-based organizations and employers use ELL Quick Start to place learners in programs or materials and to communicate information about ELL levels of proficiency.

ELL Quick Start is composed of a sequence of questions prompting replies ranging from one word, concrete replies to longer, more complex language. The level designations match those used in many schools: Beginning, Intermediate low, Intermediate high, Advanced low, and Advanced high. However, ELL Quick Start is not intended to replace formal testing.

The English Language Learning (ELL) Checklist provides a sequence of language learning common to acquiring facility in English. Language elements are checked as they are mastered. The ELL Checklist can be shared with learners, when appropriate, and passed along when the learner has a new teacher or tutor.

ENGLISH LANGUAGE LEARNING (ELL) QUICK START

Tester: _____   Student: _____

Date: _____   Address: _____

Contact Person: _____   _____

Address: _____   Phone: _____

_____   Native Country: _____

Phone: _____   Years of schooling in native country: _____

ELL level: _____ 0, _____ I, _____ II, _____ III, _____ IV

Directions: Smile. Speak clearly and slowly with normal volume. Stop after the student is unable to respond to five questions. All responses must be in spoken English. If a student has some facility in English, begin with question 6.

Hello, _____ . *My name is* _____ .
         (student)   (tester)

Oral Questions	Correct or Appropriate Responses (+)
1. How are you?	_____
2. What is this? (indicate pencil, cup, or common object)	_____
3. How many fingers? (indicate "4")	_____
4. What color is this? (indicate black, white, or yellow)	_____
5. What day of the week is this?	_____
6. How did you get here today?	_____
7. What is your favorite food?	_____
8. What do you do for fun?	_____
9. What kind of job would you like to have some day? (OR) What kind of games do you like to play?**	_____
*10. Tell me about your family (OR) Tell me about your best friend.**	_____ _____ _____
*11. What kind of material do you want to read in English? (OR) What do you like best in school?**	_____
*12. What kind of help do you want in speaking English? (OR) Tell me about your favorite TV show or movie.**	_____
*13. What kind of help do you want in writing English? (OR) Tell me what you do after school (for work).**	_____
14. (Optional) Is there something you would like to tell me or ask me?	_____

_____

_____

Thank you, _____ .
            (call student by name)

*If answers are brief, say "Please tell me more."

**Alternate question for children/adults.

If testing for ELL Quick Start began with question 6 and the student was successful on this level, give credit for the previous five items. If you overestimated the student's English facility, go back to the beginning.

Correct Responses	ELL Level	Tentative Interpretation
0–2	0 Beginning	_____ Unable to understand or respond in English
3–5	I Intermediate low	_____ Able to respond to simple questions with one- or two-word answers
6–8	II Intermediate high	_____ Able to respond to questions with simple short phrases or sentences
9–11	III Advanced low	_____ Able to produce simple discourse
12–14	IV Advanced high	_____ Able to express ideas in complex sentences with _____ fair or _____ correct structure

Observation: pronunciation is _____ good _____ fair _____ difficult to understand

Comments: _____

_____

_____

_____

_____

_____

_____

_____

Note: This test can serve as one source of information for placement of ELL students or for assistance in planning initial instruction. Teachers and tutors are encouraged to learn about the culture of their students; to obtain as much relevant information as they can from students, student contacts, or translators; and to be flexible in placement and instruction.

English Language Learning

ENGLISH LANGUAGE LEARNING (ELL) CHECKLIST

Directions: Check off communication areas and language elements as they are mastered. Topics are defined by examples.

_____ Basic expressions: yes, no, thank you, please, okay, fine

_____ Greetings: hello, good-bye, how are you

_____ Questions: who, where, when, what, why

_____ Requests: please help me, show me, tell me

_____ Names of people, places, objects

_____ Numbers, colors

_____ Vocabulary: food, restroom, health, shopping, transportation

_____ Letters and sounds of the alphabet

_____ Words for time, order, quantities, size, distance, location

_____ Word order in phrases and sentences

_____ Articles: a, an, the

_____ Conjunctions: and, but, either, or

_____ Pronouns: he, she, him, her, it, they, each, myself, ours, themselves

_____ Action verbs: run, talk, lift

_____ Forms of to be: is, are, was, am

_____ Prepositions: of, to, from, around, into, on, with, under

_____ Adjectives: large, beautiful

_____ Adverbs: quickly, beautifully

_____ Context clues to multiple meaning; homonyms: to, too, two

_____ Subject-verb agreement: he does / they do; we are / she is

_____ Pronoun-antecedent agreement: Maria / she; men / they

_____ Pronoun case agreement: subjects: we, they; objects: us, them

_____ Verb tenses: regular: _____ call, called, (have) called; _____ irregular: see, saw, (have) seen or know, knew, (have) known

_____ Compound and complex sentences

_____ Idiomatic language: change of heart; stick around

_____ Proverbs and other cultural referents

_____ Social conversation

_____ Workplace conversation

Other:

Additional assessment: The following parts of the inventory may be useful in determining student needs and planning instruction: Grammatical Clozure, Oral Language Expression, Oral Language Reception, and Written Language Expression.

Note: Although language elements are listed separately, instruction should proceed in a meaningful context such as role-playing, physical responses, and language experience. A recommended sequence is to begin in context, isolate to teach a specific skill or concept, return to context.

GRADED WORD RECOGNITION LISTS

Purpose

The Graded Word Lists tests may be used as a starting point in administering the graded reading passages, as a quick estimate of level, or to gain additional insight into the types of word recognition errors made. They may also be used to compare the student's ability to read words in isolation and in context so that information can be obtained about his or her use of experience and language clues as aids toward recognizing words.

Administration

The Graded Word Lists are included in the accompanying booklet to this text. Some teachers prefer to photocopy the lists and tape them on cards or type the lists on cards that can be laminated. Then a student can be handed the lists one at a time and is not intimidated by the large number of words on a page. Or a rectangular cutout may be made of heavy paper and used to mask all but one list at a time. If the student reads directly from the page of the test booklet, the use of a book marker may also help focus on each word. Choose the highest list on which you think the student can recognize all the words and give it to the student. Have the examiner's copy of the same list available for recording errors. If the student makes more than two errors on the first list, drop to a lower level list until no more than two errors are made. Ask the student to read consecutively higher lists until four or more words are missed. To learn more about a student's ability, the examiner may ask the student to look over words in the next highest list and read the ones known. This procedure is optional for children but recommended for adults.

Readers may not know the meanings of some words, especially if they are English language learners or lack prior knowledge. Informally assess vocabulary by asking students what some of the words mean.

Directions: Say, *"Please read these words to me. Try to say them all, even if you are not sure of some of them. Start with this list* (present it to the reader). *Use the book marker if you think it will help you keep your place."*

Recording Errors

Entry level for graded reading passages. If the only purpose in giving the word list is to estimate reading level or determine a starting point for the graded reading passages, simply record each word read correctly with a check (✓) and each word read incorrectly or not attempted with a minus (−). Self-corrections would be counted as correct.

Diagnostic purposes. If the word list is given to gain additional information about the reader's word recognition ability, a more extensive recording system is necessary. If the reader pauses before saying the word, use two checks (✓✓). Indicate words pronounced incorrectly by using diacritical marks or writing the words as pronounced. If the reader self-corrects, add a *C*. If a word part is omitted, draw a line through it. Probe vocabulary knowledge by asking the reader to define some of the words. This is especially important for those who are English language learners. Note words the reader can define as well as those that cannot be defined.

Scoring: The student's instructional level is the highest list on which no more than two errors were made. If a student missed only one word, add a half-grade level. For example, if the student missed one word on the fourth-grade list and four or more words on the fifth-grade list, indicate the level as 4.5. Two words missed on the fourth-grade list would be indicated as 4.0.

Interpretation of Errors: Ascertain additional information about the student's reading by noting whether the error occurs in the beginning, middle, or end of the word. Indicate the letter or letter combination that is mispronounced.

A comparison between the types of reading errors made in and out of context is helpful when determining a student's use of semantic, syntactic, pragmatic, and other language cues. For example, if a reader mispronounced the word *where* on the graded word list but read the sentence *Where is my dog?* correctly, the reader used other words in the sentence to recognize the unknown word. To correctly guess the word *where,* the student had to have known the remaining words *is my dog* and understood how they interrelate both semantically and syntactically. Additionally, the unknown word must have been in the reader's meaning vocabulary.

Students will usually read more words correctly when they are in context. If a student is able to pronounce words in a sentence but not on a word list, he or she has probably developed an understanding of the interrelationship of words but may have difficulty with word sound–symbol elements.

GRADED WORD LISTS

Student's Name _____   Highest instructional level (2w) _____

A	B	C	D
(PP)	(P)	(1.0)	(2.0)
____ the	____ come	____ today	____ biggest
____ am	____ you	____ does	____ where
____ get	____ went	____ three	____ yourself
____ is	____ him	____ from	____ those
____ and	____ two	____ under	____ before
____ here	____ then	____ began	____ things
____ see	____ know	____ name	____ stopped
____ not	____ around	____ there	____ place
____ can	____ pet	____ could	____ always
____ will	____ house	____ again	____ everyone

E	F	G	H
(3.0)	(4.0)	(5.0)	(6.0)
____ morning	____ important	____ because	____ aircraft
____ since	____ airport	____ bridge	____ necessary
____ together	____ through	____ microscope	____ argument
____ begin	____ fifteen	____ curious	____ chemical
____ which	____ information	____ estimation	____ representative
____ near	____ ocean	____ reliable	____ terminal
____ should	____ preview	____ government	____ apology
____ yesterday	____ laughter	____ business	____ instruction
____ eight	____ preparation	____ direction	____ evidence
____ remember	____ building	____ avenue	____ consideration

Graded Word Recognition Lists

I	J	K
(7.0)	(8.0)	(H.S.)
____ frustration	____ psychology	____ geometric
____ explanation	____ limitation	____ molecule
____ economical	____ democracy	____ editorialize
____ recognition	____ environment	____ antecedent
____ triumphant	____ barometer	____ physics
____ insignificant	____ prohibited	____ metaphorical
____ peculiar	____ relevance	____ iniquity
____ observation	____ calculate	____ extenuating
____ glossy	____ counselor	____ succinct
____ astronomer	____ endorsement	____ poignant

Graded Word Recognition Lists

USING EXPERIENTIAL WORD LISTS

One or more of the experiential word lists may be given at the discretion of the examiner. The Instructional Directions List (A) may be administered to learn whether the student can recognize words frequently encountered in instructional materials and tests. The examiner should ask the reader to describe what the word or phrase means if there is any reason to doubt his or her understanding of these tasks.

Students who lack concepts pertaining to these terms may include English language learners as well as those with little experience in formal schooling. The Experience Lists (B and C) may be administered to those students who were unable to read the preprimer level of the graded word list; List I is intended for children, and List II is intended for adults. The examiner may also ask the student what words he or she knows, print them on cards, and after a delay present them in random order. These probes are used to discover whether the student has been able to learn any words frequently encountered in daily life. The Functional Literacy List (D) may be administered to adolescents or adults who appear to be able to read above the third-grade level. One or more of the Adult Thematic Lists may be given to adults who appear to be reading on the second-grade level or above. Results of the various supplementary lists can serve as departure points for instruction if some words are known. Further assessment may be indicated in visual or auditory acuity and discrimination or vocabulary.

Research on emergent literacy (Bader & Hildebrand, 1991) focused on children's "reading" of logos, such as *McDonald's* and *Burger King.* Color logos were cut from magazines and presented to the children for identification. Later they were asked to read the words in type. Little transfer occurred. Only the words *STOP* and *KMart* were recognized in logo and type. They were the most similar in both forms. Diagnosticians may wish to use logos prominent in the environment of their children and adults to examine this capability as they test for word recognition. Adults who are functionally illiterate often state they do not try to read signs.

EXPERIENTIAL WORD LISTS

A

INSTRUCTIONAL DIRECTIONS LIST

_____ circle   _____ name

_____ match   _____ outline

_____ cross out   _____ shade

_____ underline   _____ list

_____ label   _____ complete

_____ connect   _____ number

_____ mark   _____ fill in the blank

_____ trace

B

EXPERIENCE LIST I (Children)

_____ stop   _____ push

_____ keep out   _____ walk

_____ danger   _____ park

_____ McDonald's   _____ pull

_____ boys   _____ ice cream

_____ school   _____ Pepsi-Cola

_____ girls   _____ go

_____ exit

C

EXPERIENCE LIST II (Adult)

_____ open   _____ out

_____ coffee   _____ stairs

_____ warning   _____ help wanted

_____ for rent   _____ do not cross

_____ police   _____ hospital

_____ one way   _____ for sale

_____ bus stop   _____ no smoking

_____ hot dog   _____ license

D

FUNCTIONAL LITERACY LIST

_____ address   _____ prescription

_____ telephone   _____ occupation

_____ references   _____ social security

_____ poison   _____ registration

_____ entrance   _____ emergency

_____ cashier   _____ prohibited

_____ employee   _____ deductions

Using Experiential Word Lists

ADULT THEMATIC LISTS*

The thematic lists may be used to assess adult or teen abilities to read words that share a meaningful theme. The topics health and safety, office, and vehicles offer opportunities for learners to demonstrate their strengths in one or more areas where they may have experiences. Teachers or tutors may use the words to probe vocabulary and conceptual knowledge and begin instruction in an area of learner interest.

*Adult Thematic Lists were adapted with permission from Linda Clinard, PhD, University of California, Irvine, California Reading and Literature Project.

ADULT THEMATIC LISTS

Health and Safety	Office	Vehicles
Basic	**Basic**	**Basic**
_____ cut	_____ desk	_____ brake
_____ pain	_____ form	_____ fuel
_____ fall	_____ clerk	_____ belt
_____ burn	_____ check	_____ service
_____ fever	_____ apply	_____ rough
_____ virus	_____ hire	_____ lock
_____ faint	_____ copier	_____ slow
_____ fluids	_____ receipt	_____ grease
_____ heart	_____ reply	_____ dipstick
_____ hospital	_____ message	_____ steering
Intermediate	**Intermediate**	**Intermediate**
_____ coughing	_____ business	_____ engine
_____ choking	_____ reference	_____ alternator
_____ nausea	_____ envelope	_____ generator
_____ emergency	_____ computer	_____ compression
_____ presciption	_____ manager	_____ ignition
_____ unconscious	_____ printer	_____ performance
_____ temperature	_____ accountant	_____ lubrication
_____ antiseptic	_____ receptionist	_____ distributor
_____ bacteria	_____ equipment	_____ suspension
_____ virus	_____ machinery	_____ exhaust

Using Experiential Word Lists

USING GRADED READER'S PASSAGES

In a separate booklet accompanying this text are graded reading passages. These reader passages were developed for children (C) in or near the grade-level designations spanning preprimer through twelfth grade. Passages written for children or adults are designated C/A. Passages written for adults are designated A. **Regardless of designation, select passages best suited for your students.**

The examiner's copies are intended for duplication.

Grade-Level Designation	Age Designation	Passage Title	Page No. of Examiner's Copy	Page No. of Reader's Copy
PP	C	Tip the Cat	42	10
PP	C/A	On the Bus	43	11
PP	A	The Pet Store	44	12
P	C	Lee's Friendly Meal	45	13
P	C/A	Turtles at Home	46	14
P	A	A Slippery Sidewalk	47	15
1	C	Pat and the Kitten	48	16
1	C/A	Tony and the Flower Shop	49	17
1	A	Give Me Room	50	18
2	C	The Song of Little Frog	51	19
2	C/A	Sam Buys a Newspaper	52	20
2	A	Linda at the Diner	53	21
3	C	James' Cut	54	22
3	C/A	*Today's Explorers	55	23
3	A	The Lucky Wrong Number	56	24
4	C	Checkers Game for Kim	57	25
4	C/A	The Recovery	58	26
4	A	*Land of Many Riches	59	27
5	C	Waukewa's Eagle	60	28
5	C/A	*The Nile Valley	61	29
5	A	Not in the Mood to Read	62	30
6	C	*Early Tools	63	31
6	C/A	*Constellations	64	32
6	A	*Driver's Licenses	65	33
7	C	*Volcanoes	66	34
7	C/A	*Questions about Dinosaurs	67	35
7	A	The Job Application	68	36
8	C	*Kon-Tiki	69	37
8	C/A	A Shopping Trip	70	38
8	A	A New Job	71	39
9–10	C	*Modern Chemistry	72	40
9–10	C/A	*A Failure to Communicate	73	41
9–10	A	Voter Drive	74	42
11–12	C	*Impressionists	75	43
11–12	C/A	*Global Warfare	76	44
11–12	A	*Improvement for Workers	77	45

*Number of expository passages increase with level of difficulty for all categories.

GRADED READER'S PASSAGES

Reading and Listening Levels

The major objective in using the Graded Reader Passages is to estimate the reader's instructional level for placement in materials. The instructional level is defined as the level on which a learner is challenged but not frustrated. Accurate word recognition and comprehension are taken into consideration. The examiner is given the option of having the student sight read aloud after a brief introduction or read silently before reading aloud. These conditions are termed *unprepared* and *prepared* reading

Grade Levels Primer–Third

Accuracy		*Comprehension*
Prepared oral reading: 95%	Unprepared oral reading: 90%	Depending on detail, memories: 60%–70%

Grade Levels Fourth and Above

Accuracy		*Comprehension*
Prepared oral reading: 98%	Unprepared oral reading: 95%	Depending on detail, memories: 60%–70%

The three sets of graded passages indicated as C (child), C/A (child/adult), or A (adult) are to be used to obtain an instructional reading level based on responses after oral and silent reading. An instructional *listening comprehension* level can also be obtained by evaluating responses of the student after hearing passages read aloud by the examiner. Minimum level of memories after listening is 60% for instructional level.

The 60% figure under Comprehension does not mean the reader understands only 60% of what was read or heard. Rather, this figure refers to a percentage of ideas recalled, mostly literal details, and represents a higher level of comprehension than 60% according to research.

It seems reasonable to assume that more difficult materials will usually result in frustration for the student and that easier materials can be read by the student independently of teacher support. Therefore, the examiner is not burdened with percentages for these level designations. Understanding and recall for specific passages are affected by the prior knowledge and interest of the reader. These factors must be considered when estimating the ability of a particular student to comprehend various materials.

Examiners do not have to compute percentages. An instructional-level guide is provided with each passage.

Determining a Starting Point

Results from either the Graded Word List test or from school records are used to determine a starting point for the graded passages. Within each level, choose the passage—designated for children (C), children or adults (C/A), or adults (A)—that appears to be most suited to the reader regardless of age. What is most important is to choose a passage that the reader might find the most interesting or appealing. Select the highest level passage that the student would appear to be able to read independently. If school records, for example, indicate that a student is having moderate difficulty reading fifth-grade-level material, start the graded passages at a second-grade level. If the selected passage is too difficult, move down until the independent level is found. Proceed with more difficult material until the student reaches a frustration level.

If information about level of functioning is absent, administer the Graded Word List test. Have the student begin reading the graded passages one level below the highest level on which no more than two words were missed on the Graded Word List test, or the highest independent level. If a student, for example, missed one word on the first-, second-, and third-grade lists and two words on the fourth-grade list, start the graded passages at the third-grade level. Have the student continue reading more advanced graded passages until the frustration level is reached.

Oral Reading

Unprepared versus Prepared Oral Reading: The unprepared oral reading condition can save time during testing and can give the examiner information on the reader's ability to instantly recognize words and process ideas. However, some students have difficulty in oral expression and need an opportunity to read silently before reading aloud in order to give a more accurate display of their abilities to recognize words. Either condition may be used at the examiner's discretion.

Directions for Oral Reading: In each form, the examiner's copy will include a statement with a question to assess the reader's prior knowledge and a motivating statement. For both unprepared and prepared oral reading, first read the title of the passage to the student. Next read the statement and question to assess the reader's prior knowledge. If prior knowledge appears inadequate, select an alternative passage from a different form.

Unprepared Oral Reading: Say to the student, *"Here are some passages I would like you to read. Please read this one aloud. Try to remember what you read so that you might be able to tell me about it or answer questions about the passage."* Finally, read the motivating statement that accompanies each passage to develop a purpose for reading.

Prepared Oral Reading: Say, *"Here are some passages I would like you to read. Please read this one silently to yourself. Tell me when you have finished; then I will have you read it to me. Try to remember what you read so that you might be able to tell me about it or answer questions about the passage."* Finally, read the motivating statement that accompanies each passage to develop a purpose for reading.

As the student reads aloud, record the performance by using the coding guidelines in this section or a code that is familiar to you. Check appropriate blanks with regard to meaningful word substitutions, rate, and fluency. The kinds of oral reading inaccuracies, if they are numerous, may be marked after the student has departed. Repeat this procedure with higher level passages until the student has failed to meet the minimum requirements for oral reading accuracy as indicated at the end of each passage page.

Recording and Scoring Oral Reading Performance: Miscues (oral reading errors) can be evaluated both quantitatively and qualitatively. In order to determine the reading levels quickly, instructors should perform a quantitative analysis that gives consideration to evidence of frustration. Fluency will be analyzed qualitatively to assist in instruction.

Quantitative Analysis

A quantitative analysis focuses on the number of deviations from the printed text. These include substitutions, insertions, omissions, repetitions, words unknown, dialect, and self-corrections. As the student reads aloud, record the performance, count the miscues, and use the total to determine the student's reading level along with comprehension.

Try to tape record the student's reading, if it is not a disturbance, and check the accuracy by coding performance at a later time. The major purpose of recording performance during oral reading is to analyze the reader's strengths as well as difficulties as he or she attempts to use oral language in extracting meaning from printed language. Therefore, all deviations from the texts are to be recorded even though they may not be considered as errors.

With the exception of beginning readers, most students will have better recall after silent reading than after oral reading. The purpose of oral reading is to ascertain the student's strengths and weaknesses in oral reading miscues. Therefore, for most students reading beyond the primary level, comprehension assessment may be omitted after oral reading. Conversely, students reading below the third-grade level may have better comprehension after oral reading. Giving an oral reading and a silent reading passage at every level can be time-consuming and stressful for the student, but may be done at the examiner's discretion.

When the frustration level is reached for oral reading (one level above the highest instructional level), begin silent reading with an alternative passage on the student's highest instructional level during oral reading.

The following code and scoring guidelines are recommended.

Code and Scoring Guidelines of Graded Reader's Passages

Behavior	Coding	Example	Scoring
1. Substitutions and mispronunciations that disrupt meaning	Write the response above the word	*gaged* she gazed at it	1
2. Substitutions, mispronunciations, and inversions that do not disrupt meaning	Write the response above the word; draw curved line for inversions	*looked* she gazed at it	0
		"I saw him," Mary said.	0
3. Repeated substitutions or mispronunciations for same word	Write response each time, but count one error	*wafer* the water was	1
		. . . then the *wafer* water flowed	
4. Insertions	Write the word with a caret	*little* a ∧ dog	1
5. Omissions and partial omissions	Draw a line through word or word part omitted	the ~~tall~~ girl	1
		walki~~ng~~ on	1
6. Words pronounced by the examiner	Wait at least five seconds; write *P* above aided word	*P* I thought	1

Behavior	Coding	Example	Scoring
7. Repetitions of words or phrases	Write *R* above each repetition; draw a line over the words repeated; score as 1 regardless of repetitions	R R̄ the cat howled	1

Record but do not score the following:

Behavior	Coding	Example	Scoring
8. Self-corrections	Write *C* above corrections	C went I want to	0
9. Repetitions to make corrections	As above	C I want to went I want to	0
10. Hesitations	Put a check above each hesitation	√ He thought	0
11. Substitutions and mispronunciations resulting from a dialect	Write the deviation from the text, if there is time	be goin She goes every day	0
12. Ignored punctuation	Put an *X* over disregarded punctuation	the car X Then	0
13. Phrasing	Insert lines to indicate phrasing, if there is time	the / car / came down the street	0

In the sentence "*She gazed at it,*" the student substituted *gaged* for *gazed* in example 1 and *looked* for *gazed* in example 2. Since *gaged* and *gazed* have very different meanings, the meaning of the sentence is changed. However, the substitution of *looked* for *gazed* does not distort the meaning of the passage. Therefore, the reading behavior in example 1 is scored one point, while the reading behavior in example 2 is scored a zero.

In example 3, the reader substitutes the word *wafer* for *water* twice in the same passage. Because both incorrect responses are identical, the examiner counts only one miscue, not two. Count consistent mispronunciations of a word several times in a passage only once.

Occasionally, a student may omit several words together or even an entire line. If this occurs, count the omission as only one miscue.

Qualitative Analysis and Instruction

How are student errors analyzed?

To gain information required for planning appropriate reading instruction, it is necessary to go beyond quantititive results and analyze the test results qualitatively. Knowing a student's strengths and needs in relation to reading for meaning is essential for planning an effective instructional program. Analysis proceeds through examination of the student's processing of language components. Mercer and Mercer (2001) explain that language components are distinct but interrelated and interactive. The components are phonology, morphology, syntax, semantics, and pragmatics.

According to Goodman (1969), the quality of reading responses should be analyzed in terms of the reader's reliance on three cueing systems: grapho-phonic, syntactic, and semantic cues. A fourth cueing system, pragmatics, refers to the social use of language and also affects reading.

How do cueing systems differ?

Grapho-phonic cues refer to the relationship between the grapheme (letter) and the phoneme (smallest unit of sound). If the word *horse* is substituted for *house,* the reader is using grapho-phonic elements of the text, because the words look and sound similar. If, however, the word substituted was *cabin* for *house,* the reader would not be using grapho-phonic cues, because there is no sound-symbol similarity between the two words.

Syntactic cues are obtained from the grammar of the language. If the sentence "*I fed the dog*" was read "*I bought the dog,*" the reader is using syntactic cues. By correctly substituting a verb, the reader shows an understanding of the language. If, however, the same sentence is read "*I friend the dog,*" syntactic cues are not used because the reader incorrectly substitutes a noun for a verb. In this example, the reader finds the material too difficult to use knowledge of language structure.

Semantic cues are derived from the meaning of the sentence. They are obtained from the semantic content of what is read. If the sentence "*I feel great*" was read "*I feel terrific,*" the reader used semantic cues and is on his or her way to being a successful reader. Semantic cues would not have been used if the same sentence were read "*I feel bad.*" The reader missed the idea of the author; therefore, the substitution did not keep the original meaning of the sentence.

When a reader uses known words in a sentence to help recognize an unknown word, he or she is relying on semantic or syntactic cues. It is impossible to use semantic cues without using syntactic cues. If the substitution is semantically correct, it must also be syntactically correct. However, the reverse does not apply. It is possible for a substitution to be syntactically but not semantically correct. An example of this would be substituting the word *built* for *bought* in the sentence, "*I bought a bicycle.*"

Pragmatic cues reflect social usage such as dialect. A boy who used farm equipment read the phrase "stepped on the brakes" as "pulled on the brakes" because he was accustomed to using the word *pull* in his work.

What are the steps involved in a qualitative analysis?

A qualitative analysis is predicated on administering an Informal Reading Inventory and attending to the cue system of the student. In order for the examiner to focus on patterns of performance and types of miscues, the student must orally read passages of varying difficulty.

How may oral reading performance indicate a student's reading strategy?

Summarizing all oral reading miscues on a master sheet will yield specific information about a student's reading strategies as well as strengths and weaknesses. The following questions, encompassing the three cue systems, should serve as a guide:

1. Does the reader use grapho-phonic strategies?
2. Which specific grapho-phonic elements are known? Which ones are unknown?
3. Is word length related to accuracy? Does the student pronounce a grapho-phonic element correctly in small words but not in larger ones?
4. Are miscues made in the beginning, middle, or end of the word?
5. Is the problem with structural analysis? What specific prefixes and suffixes are known? Which ones are unknown?
6. Can the student use context clues to figure out unknown words?
7. Does the reader have difficulty with particular grammatical functions (verb, adverb, noun)?
8. Does the miscue interfere with comprehension?
9. Is the sentence containing the miscue semantically acceptable, or is there a change in meaning?
10. Does the reader correct the miscue and make the sentence semantically acceptable?
11. What are the most common patterns of performance?
12. Has the reader made dialect substitutions that make sense?

How does the analysis of student errors serve as a guide for goal setting?

After answering the previous questions, make a list of the student's known strengths and instructional needs. Maintain an accounting of the student's knowledge by recording both the text and the miscue. Note whether each miscue is graphically or phonetically similar in the beginning, middle, or end of the original word. Then determine if the miscue is either syntactically or semantically acceptable. Analyze a number of miscues to find a pattern of performance. Note, for example whether the reader uses grapho-phonic cues, especially in the beginning and end of the word. If, of the miscues, only two are syntactically and one semantically correct. Consequently, we can conclude that the reader is not using context. The instructional program should address this area. To design lessons, directly translate this information into instructional objectives. Lessons that start with strengths and proceed to the teaching of needed skills are more meaningful to students. For example, when teaching grapheme-phoneme and structural analysis relationships, it is advantageous to start with words known by sight because students can already relate to them. As skills are mastered, adjust the list of strengths and instructional needs for each student so that the evaluation remains current.

Is there a recommended strategy for remediation of grapho-phonic cues?

One successful strategy is the inductive teaching of grapho-phonic elements. The following procedure is suggested.

Objective: Grapheme-Phoneme Relationship of *bl*

1. Determine that the prerequisite skills of auditory and visual discrimination have been acquired.
2. Select several words that the students already know by sight that contain the grapho-phonic element to be taught. Write the words in 2 columns. Have the students read the words.

blue	blanket
blend	blank

3. Ask the students, *"How are all these words alike?"* The students must establish two things: They all start with *bl* letters. They all start with the sound one hears at the beginning of *black.*

4. Read the words to the students while they listen for the letters that represent the /bl/ sound.

5. Ask the students to think of additional words that start with the same sound they hear in *blue, blend, blanket, blank.* Write these additional words under *blank* (the final word on the list).

6. Have students read all the words in the list. Direct them to look at the first two letters and note the beginning sound of the word.

7. To apply the sound-symbol association, students must know the sound the letters represent and be able to blend it with other sounds to produce an entire word. To teach students to blend, begin with a known phonogram (*ake, ack, ink*). If necessary, teach the phonogram by sight. Then place the *bl* in front of the phonogram and have the student pronounce the new word.

8. Students must have the opportunity to practice their new skill in reading. Give students appropriate reading material (instructional level) and have them circle and read all the words that begin with *bl.*

What strategies aid students' use of semantic and syntactic cues?

One reason students ignore semantic and syntactic cues is due to the difficulty of the material. If vocabulary, sentence structure, and concepts are incomprehensible, the reader will be unable to use context effectively. Consequently, the first task is to see if easier or more interesting material corrects the problem. If these adjustments work, it is imperative to provide the students practice time with reading material that is on the appropriate level and matches their interests. However, if students continue to make substitutions that do not keep the meaning of the sentence, proceed with instruction in simple closure activities. Make students aware of the language's syntactic and semantic cue systems by giving them the following activities.

1. Place a paragraph written on the student's independent reading level on the overhead. Select one part of speech, such as a verb, and cover several verbs in the paragraph with a slip of paper.

2. Proceed with one verb at a time, and discuss with students additional words that fit in the blank and maintain the meaning of the sentence.

3. Place several student responses on the overhead, and discuss whether they are appropriate. Focus on how the other words in the same sentence supply cues.

4. Emphasize that cues may be obtained from other sentences and paragraphs.

5. Continue the practice with other parts of speech. Initially implement the activities using teacher-directed, whole-group lessons. Eventually use cooperative student groups. These same types of activities can be used individually when students are silently reading.

Silent Reading and Listening Comprehension

Directions for Silent Reading: As with oral reading, assess the student's background knowledge. If adequate, say to the student, *"Now I will ask you to read passages silently and then tell me what you have read or answer questions about what you read."* Continue by reading the motivating statement to the student. When the student has finished, take the passage from him or her.

Comprehension should be assessed after silent reading by using unprompted memories, direct questions, or a combination. With unprompted memories the student retells all the information remembered about the passage. Encourage the student to continue by asking such general questions as, *"Can you think of something else? What else happened? Tell me more."* Also probe by asking a specific question related to the student's response. When a reader, for example, answers, "The bird was brought in for the little girl to care for," ask, *"What did the little girl do then?"* or *"What happened to the bird?"* When probing, be certain not to supply the reader with any information that is contained in the passage.

The advantage of unprompted memories is that some readers prefer to tell what they remember rather than be asked pinpointed questions. As they retell the passage, they may remember other facts through association. If students are asked initially to answer questions and are unable to remember, they may become nervous. By asking the student to recall anything remembered about the passage, the examiner is starting with the student's strengths.

Students who have difficulty processing, retrieving, and organizing the information from the passage may require direct questioning. For them, using a combination of unprompted memories and direct questioning is probably best for assessing comprehension. Start by asking the student to simply retell the passage. **If insufficient memories are given, note any missing information and use direct questioning to ascertain whether the student has difficulty retrieving or comprehending the material.**

List the memories accurately recalled as they occur (1-2-3, etc.). On the lower level passages, a list of possible unprompted memories is supplied with the comprehension questions. On the upper level passages, use the answers to the questions as a guide, and list order of memories in front of the questions answered. **Use the questions to prompt recall of information not given in retelling if the number of recalled memories is inadequate.** When the total number of memories from retelling and/or questioning equals the number required on the guide, stop. Retelling, or answers that paraphrase the meaning or wording of the passage, are to be considered correct. As a further probe of the student's ability, the examiner may permit the reader to reinspect the passage to find the answer to a question. Note whether the reader can scan to find information. The interpretive questions are not counted in the total number of memories. If the first passage is too difficult, go to a lower level passage. Continue with the silent reading of higher level passages until the student cannot meet the minimum requirements for silent reading comprehension.

Listening Comprehension: Say to the student, *"Now I will read passages to you. Please listen so that you can tell me what you heard or answer questions about what you heard."* Begin with an alternative passage on the highest instructional level achieved under the silent reading procedure, and continue reading aloud higher level passages until the student cannot meet the minimum requirements for listening comprehension.

Interpreting and Summarizing the Results of the Graded Passages

To convert the raw score into a reading level, the teacher should consult the instructional-level guide at the bottom of the examiner's copy of each graded passage. Separate limits are available for both prepared and unprepared oral reading. Select the limit for the appropriate circumstance, and compare that figure to the total number of miscues the reader made. If the total number of miscues is within the designated limit, the student has not reached the instructional level. Continue having the student read until the frustration level for word recognition is determined.

The student's highest instructional level for word recognition is used as a starting point for comprehension assessment. After the student has read the passage silently, count the total number of both prompted and unprompted memories. Compare this total to the criteria established in each instructional level guide. If the number of memories matches or exceeds the limit established, continue having the student read more difficult passages silently until the highest instructional level for comprehension is reached. Many readers have better recall of narrative passages than of expository passages. Performance on both types of passages may be evaluated if time permits.

Record the highest instructional levels achieved by the student on the summary sheets under *Reading profile,* oral, silent, and listening designations. Examine the scoring sheets and consider all of the reading behaviors of the student. A great deal can be inferred about comprehension from oral reading. A lack of inflection, word-by-word reading, or inappropriate inflection and emphasis may indicate poor comprehension. Inappropriate substitutions, in particular, may indicate difficulties, whereas good substitutions indicate the converse. It is well to remember, however, that these are inferences. Some flat, word-by-word oral readers are competent in comprehension.

Generally, the student's instructional level should be the highest level passage in which there is adequate comprehension in silent reading. However, if the student's reading is extremely slow, the instructional level may be one level lower than the passage on which comprehension was adequate. The term *instructional level* as used here refers to an instructional condition in which the teacher is giving direct aid, support, and guidance. In some instructional settings, students are expected to work independently of the teacher; they may be asked to read and answer questions, complete worksheets, or follow directions without assistance. This is termed *independent learning level* and should be about one level below the instructional level for levels P–5 and two levels below for 6–12. Estimation of independent learning level should be made by someone familiar with the instructional program in which the student will be placed.

The listening comprehension level may be used as an estimate of current potential and indicates the student's capacity for understanding what is heard.

To a great extent, teacher judgment is required in placing students in materials because many factors beyond word recognition and comprehension are important. For example, a student may be given some easy materials to read for a time in order to build fluency, rate, or confidence. Conversely, a student may be permitted to proceed in difficult materials because of a strong interest in the content. Stages of reading development, age, interests, learning rate, and personality are factors that need to be considered as a teacher chooses between the hazards of frustrating a student with difficult materials and not challenging her or him by using easy materials.

In addition to the determination of level or levels of placement, the reader's performance on the graded passages can be analyzed as to strengths and weaknesses to be considered in planning instruction. The summary sheets contain checklists where information from graded passages, word lists, phonics, and other tests can be combined and recommendations made for instruction.

EXAMPLE OF TESTING FOR INSTRUCTIONAL LEVEL
Jeff, a fourth-grade student

1. Graded Word List: missed 1 word,   1.0
   missed 1 word,   2.0
   missed 3 words, 3.0
   GWL level: 2.5

2. Unprepared Oral Reading

2C/A—   1 repetition
                 1 substitution that did change meaning
                 2 substitutions that did not change meaning

Rate appeared to be average. Answer to interpretive question: "Well, this was probably one of those import-type places where the owner was Greek and kept Greek food and things for other Greek people and people who like Greek food. He walked a long way and didn't know where he was."

3C/A—   3 mispronunciations that disrupted meaning
                 1 word pronounced by examiner
                 2 substitutions that did not change meaning
                 1 insertion

Rate was slow. Answer to interpretive question: "I guess they like to be famous, and they see neat things."

3. Silent Reading

2A—Retelling: 8 memories, in sequence

Rate was average. Answer to interpretive question: "She probably was a dropout and wants to finish. My brother went to school like that."

3A—Retelling: 8 memories, in sequence

Rate was average. Answer to interpretive question: "If there wasn't a wrong number, they wouldn't know where he moved to."

4A—Retelling: 4 memories, not in sequence
Questioning: 1 memory from questioning

Rate appeared to be slow. Much whispering, making faces. Answer to interpretive question: "Well, if you are rich, you are the best."

4. Listening

Ordinarily the examiner would start with an instructional-level passage, but because Jeff appeared to have good language development, he was given a passage on the fourth level.

4C—Retelling: 7 memories, in sequence

Answer to interpretive question: "It makes you mad at yourself when you can't do things. I get like that."

5C—Retelling: 7 memories, in sequence

Answer to interpretive question: "Sometimes they can tell you're their friend. You can't trust wild animals, though."

(Jeff did not reach frustration in listening until the seventh-grade level.)

5. Recommended instructional level for materials placement: 3.0
Independent learning level in reading materials: 2.0–2.5
Frustration level: 4.0
Current potential: 6.0 (listening comprehension level)

Differences in Word List and Passages Performance

Determining an appropriate instructional level when the Graded Word List and Passages results are significantly different depends on language facility and other factors. Here are some examples:

Maria, a sixth-grade student

Maria attended grades one through five in Mexico. She has been in the United States for six months and has just entered a new school. Her English level was estimated at the intermediate low level (1). She could respond to simple questions with one- or two-word answers.

Graded Word List Level: 4.0   Passages Level: Preprimer

Maria was able to read in Spanish. She could pronounce English words because of phonetic similarities to Spanish, but she did not know the meaning of the words. Her English vocabulary has to be developed. She may be instructed to read English with the language experience approach. She should be placed in preprimer materials with only a few words per page and pictures that are appealing to her interests.

Ahmed, a high school junior

Ahmed has been in the United States for one year. Because of moves from the Sudan to Kenya to the United States, his education has been disrupted. He can read in Arabic. His English level was estimated at advanced low (3). He was able to produce simple discourse correctly and easily, but his written expression revealed sentence fragments and tense shifts.

Graded Word List Level: 4.0   Passages Level: 6.0

Ahmed was able to read a sixth-grade-level passage silently with comprehension because he was able to use his background knowledge and context to decode words and unlock the meaning of unfamiliar words. However, his rate was quite slow. He needs practice in fourth- and fifth-grade-level material to build fluency. He can use sixth-grade-level material with an instructor's assistance in guided reading if the reading assignment is brief.

Will, a fourth-grade student

Will speaks no other language but English. He appears to have no visual, auditory, or language difficulties. He was assessed because his academic performance was poor.

Graded Word List Level: 4.0   Passages Level: 2

Will had very poor recall on the third-grade-level passages. He read passages orally and silently at a very fast rate (150 and 200 wpm). In a follow-up discussion with Will, he repeated his belief that getting done fast meant he was good at school work. Will was helped to understand the need to read for meaning and given guidance in purpose setting and taking responsibility to verify his recollections.

Determining Instructional Levels

- Although passages have instructional-level guides for numbers of errors and memories, the examiner is encouraged to consider all aspects of behavior to decide on an instructional level. For example, a reader may meet the quantified specifications, but be extremely slow. In that case, go down a level. Practice on a lower level may build fluency and confidence.

- The prepared oral reading condition is highly recommended for English language learners and for students with language processing disabilities, such as slow oral language retrieval.

- Choose passages the learner seems to have sufficient background to comprehend. You may ignore the labels indicating passages for children (C), for children or adults (C/A), and for adults (A). This is especially important for English language learners. You may give the learner a brief explanation to build background before reading if you do not give away the specifics of the passage. Comprehension of narrative passages is usually better than comprehension of expository passages.

- Remember to explain to the students they will be asked to tell what was read or to answer questions. When a child was asked to tell what she read, she said, "I don't know. I wasn't listening to me." She did well on retelling when she understood she was expected to recall the content.

- Number the items in the order they were recalled to obtain evidence of organizational sequencing.

- Do not ask listed questions if retelling has provided enough memories. When retelling has not produced enough memories, ask the questions not already answered in retelling. Stop when the total of unprompted memories in retelling and the prompted memories from answering the questions meet the instructional-level guide at the bottom of each page. Following this procedure will result in less stress for the learner and save time.

- Retelling or responding to questions may be omitted after oral reading for upper-level readers who generally have better recall after silent reading.

- The instructional-level guide for each passage has been carefully researched and verified by professional reviewers. There is no need to compute percentages to determine instructional level. The frustration level is one above the instructional level, and the independent level is one lower than the instructional level. Regardless if percentages are computed, one must take into account the learner's language abilities and confidence. For this reason, reliance on traditional computation of instructional, frustration, and independent levels is not justified.

- The best determination of instructional level includes performance on the graded word list and passages in addition to language facility.

- The word list alone usually gives an accurate instructional level for students who are not English language learners or do not have language processing difficulties or other disabilities.

- You may opt to permit students to look back in a passage to learn if they can quickly and accurately locate information.

- You may opt to give students questions in writing and permit them to write the answers if, for example, they have an auditory processing difficulty or have had English language instruction that has not emphasized oral language.

- Give students an opportunity to tell you what their strengths are and what kind of instruction they would like to receive. Ask them what they think about their performance on the various tests.

GRADED PASSAGE (PPC)

Assessing and Activating Background Knowledge

Here is a story about a cat. What do cats like to do?

_____ Adequate   _____ Inadequate

Motivating Statement   *Read the story to find out what kind of a pet this is and what things it likes to do.*

TIP THE CAT

Tip is a cat.

She likes to eat fish.

She is a fat cat.

Tip eats fish and sleeps.

She likes to sit on my lap.

She is a good pet.   (31 words)

Unprompted Memories   **Comprehension Questions**

Please retell the story.   _____ *What kind of animal is the story about?*   (cat)

_____ cat   _____ *What is the animal's name?*   (Tip)

_____ named Tip   _____ *What does Tip eat?*   (fish)

_____ likes fish   _____ *What does Tip do?*   (eats)

_____ fat cat   _____ (sleeps)

_____ sleeps and eats fish   _____ *Where does Tip like to sit?*   (lap)

_____ sits on lap   _____ *What kind of pet is Tip?*   (good or cat)

_____ good pet

Interpretive question: *Why do you think Tip is fat?*

    Acceptable answer: _____ Yes _____ No

Memories: _____ Unprompted + _____ Prompted = _____ Total

Organized retelling: _____ Yes _____ No

Oral reading inaccuracies changed meaning: _____ Yes _____ No

Rate appropriate: _____ Yes _____ No   Fluency appropriate: _____ Yes _____ No

    _____ reads word by word   _____ reads in phrases   _____ good use of punctuation

    _____ good use of stress, pitch, and intonation

Oral reading:

    _____ Substitutions   _____ Mispronunciations

    _____ Additions   _____ Repetitions

    _____ Omissions   _____ Words pronounced by examiner

INSTRUCTIONAL-LEVEL GUIDE   **Prepared: 2 or fewer errors   Unprepared: 3 or fewer errors   5 or more memories**

GRADED PASSAGE (PPC/A)

Assessing and Activating Background Knowledge

Here is a story about some people on a bus. What is it like for you to ride on a bus?

_____ Adequate   _____ Inadequate

Motivating Statement   *Read the story to find out about a bus ride.*

ON THE BUS

We are going home.

Stop and go.

Stop and go.

The bus is so slow.

Look at that man.

He has a bike.

He can go fast.   (27 words)

Unprompted Memories

Please retell the story.

_____ we are going home

_____ stop and go, stop and go

_____ look at that man

_____ has a bike

_____ can go fast

Comprehension Questions

_____ *Where were people going?*   (home)

_____ *How was the bus moving?*   (stop and go or slow)

_____ *What did the people on the bus look at?*   (a man)

_____ *What did the man have?*   (a bike)

_____ *How was the man riding?*   (on a bike, or fast)

Interpretive question: *Why is the bus so slow?*

Acceptable answer: _____ Yes _____ No

Memories: _____ Unprompted + _____ Prompted = _____ Total

Organized retelling: _____ Yes _____ No

Oral reading inaccuracies changed meaning: _____ Yes _____ No

Rate appropriate: _____ Yes _____ No   Fluency appropriate: _____ Yes _____ No

_____ reads word by word   _____ reads in phrases   _____ good use of punctuation

_____ good use of stress, pitch, and intonation

Oral reading:

_____ Substitutions   _____ Mispronunciations

_____ Additions   _____ Repetitions

_____ Omissions   _____ Words pronounced by examiner

INSTRUCTIONAL-LEVEL GUIDE   Prepared: 1 or fewer errors   Unprepared: 3 or fewer errors   3 or more memories

GRADED PASSAGE (PPA)

Assessing and Activating Background Knowledge

This is a story about a pet store. Tell me what you know about pet stores.

_____ Adequate   _____ Inadequate

Motivating Statement   *Read the story to find out about the different dogs at the pet store.*

THE PET STORE

I went to a pet store.

I saw big dogs.

I saw little dogs.

I saw dogs with long hair.

I saw dogs with short hair.

I got a little dog.   (31 words)

Unprompted Memories	**Comprehension Questions**
Please retell the story.	_____ *Where did the person go?* (pet store)
_____ pet store	_____ *What size were the dogs?* (big)
_____ big dogs	_____ (little)
_____ little dogs	_____ *What was their hair like?* (long)
_____ long hair	_____ (short)
_____ short hair	_____ *What kind of dog was bought?* (little)
_____ got a dog	

Interpretive question: *What other pets are found in pet stores?*

   Acceptable answer: _____ Yes   _____ No

Memories: _____ Unprompted + _____ Prompted = _____ Total

Organized retelling: _____ Yes   _____ No

Oral reading inaccuracies changed meaning: _____ Yes _____ No

Rate appropriate: _____ Yes _____ No   Fluency appropriate: _____ Yes _____ No

   _____ reads word by word   _____ reads in phrases   _____ good use of punctuation

   _____ good use of stress, pitch, and intonation

Oral reading:

   _____ Substitutions   _____ Mispronunciations

   _____ Additions   _____ Repetitions

   _____ Omissions   _____ Words pronounced by examiner

INSTRUCTIONAL-LEVEL GUIDE   Prepared: 1 or fewer errors   Unprepared: 3 or fewer errors   4 or more memories

GRADED PASSAGE (PC)

Assessing and Activating Background Knowledge

Here is a story about a fish. What do you know about fish?

_____ Adequate   _____ Inadequate

Motivating Statement   *Read about this special fish and find out what he does and how he lives.*

LEE'S FRIENDLY MEAL

Lee was a little blue fish.

Some of his friends were very big fish.

Lee's big friends lived far away.

But he saw them every day.

Every day they would swim by to see Lee.

Tiny animals lived on the big fish.

Lee ate the tiny animals.

This made the big fish happy.   (53 words)

Unprompted Memories

Please retell the story.

_____ Lee the fish
_____ little, blue
_____ friends are big fish
_____ they lived far away
_____ swim to see Lee every day
_____ Lee ate little animals
_____ off big fish
_____ big fish happy

Comprehension Questions

_____ *Who was Lee?*   (fish)
_____ *What did Lee look like?*   (little)
_____ (blue)
_____ *Who were Lee's friends?*   (big fish)
_____ *Where did his friends live?*   (far away)
_____ *When did his friends come to see Lee?*   (every day)
_____ *What did Lee do when they came?*   (ate little animals)
_____ *How did the big fish feel after Lee's meal?*   (happy)

Interpretive question: *Why did the big fish feel happy after Lee ate the little animals that lived on them?*

Acceptable answer: _____ Yes _____ No

Memories: _____ Unprompted + _____ Prompted = _____ Total

Organized retelling: _____ Yes _____ No

Oral reading inaccuracies changed meaning: _____ Yes _____ No

Rate appropriate: _____ Yes _____ No   Fluency appropriate: _____ Yes _____ No

_____ reads word by word   _____ reads in phrases   _____ good use of punctuation
_____ good use of stress, pitch, and intonation

Oral reading:

_____ Substitutions   _____ Mispronunciations
_____ Additions   _____ Repetitions
_____ Omissions   _____ Words pronounced by examiner

INSTRUCTIONAL-LEVEL GUIDE Prepared: 3 or fewer errors   Unprepared: 5 or fewer errors   5 or more memories

GRADED PASSAGE (PC/A)

Assessing and Activating Background Knowledge

Here is a story about turtles. What do you know about turtles?

_____ Adequate   _____ Inadequate

Motivating Statement   *Read the story to learn about turtles and why they are always at home.*

TURTLES AT HOME

Turtles are always at home.

If they visit the sea, they are at home.

If they go to the high hills, they are at home.

If they go far away, they have a home.

Turtles carry their homes with them.

Their shell is their house.

Turtles stay in their shells.

That is why they are always at home.   (58 words)

Unprompted Memories

Please retell the story.

_____ turtles at home

_____ visit sea, at home

_____ go to hills, at home

_____ go far away, have a home

_____ carry their home

_____ shell is a house

_____ stay in their shell

_____ why always home

Comprehension Questions

_____ *When are turtles at home?*   (always at home)

_____ *Where do turtles visit?*   (high hills)

_____ (sea)

_____ (far away)

_____ *What do the turtles carry all the time?*   (own home or shell)

_____ *What is the turtle's house?*   (his shell)

Interpretive question: *Why don't turtles leave their shells?*

       Acceptable answer: _____ Yes _____ No

Memories: _____ Unprompted + _____ Prompted = _____ Total

Organized retelling: _____ Yes _____ No

Oral reading inaccuracies changed meaning: _____ Yes _____ No

Rate appropriate: _____ Yes _____ No   Fluency appropriate: _____ Yes _____ No

       _____ reads word by word   _____ reads in phrases   _____ good use of punctuation

       _____ good use of stress, pitch, and intonation

Oral reading:

       _____ Substitutions   _____ Mispronunciations

       _____ Additions   _____ Repetitions

       _____ Omissions   _____ Words pronounced by examiner

INSTRUCTIONAL-LEVEL GUIDE   Prepared: 3 or fewer errors   Unprepared: 6 or fewer errors   5 or more memories

Using Graded Reader's Passages

GRADED PASSAGE (PA)

Assessing and Activating Background Knowledge

Here is a story about a slippery sidewalk. What problems can be caused by a slippery sidewalk?

_____ Adequate   _____ Inadequate

Motivating Statement   *Read the story to learn about the problems caused by this slippery sidewalk and what was done about it.*

A SLIPPERY SIDEWALK

It was a cold day.

A man fell on the ice.

He was not hurt.

"Put salt on the ice," said Bill.

"Salt will melt the ice."

"Salt can kill the grass," said Pat.

"Put sand on the ice."

"I will try to find some sand," said Bill.

"But it is better to kill some grass than

have a bad fall."   (61 words)

Unprompted Memories

Please retell the story.

_____ cold day

_____ man fell on ice, not hurt

_____ put salt on ice (Bill)

_____ salt kills grass (Pat)

_____ put sand on ice (Pat)

_____ will find some sand (Bill)

_____ better to kill grass than to have a bad fall

Comprehension Questions

_____ *What kind of day was it?*   (cold)

_____ *What happened to the man?*   (fell on ice)

_____ *How was the man after the fall?*   (not hurt)

_____ *What did Bill say?*   (put salt on ice)

_____ *Why did Bill say use salt?*   (to melt ice)

_____ *Why did Pat say not to use salt?*   (kills grass)

_____ *What did Pat want to use?*   (sand)

_____ *What did Bill decide?*   (to find sand)

Interpretive question: *Why was Bill more concerned about people falling on the ice than about killing the grass?*

    Acceptable answer: _____ Yes _____ No

Memories: _____ Unprompted + _____ Prompted = _____ Total

Organized retelling: _____ Yes _____ No

Oral reading inaccuracies changed meaning: _____ Yes _____ No

Rate appropriate: _____ Yes _____ No   Fluency appropriate: _____ Yes _____ No

    _____ reads word by word   _____ reads in phrases   _____ good use of punctuation

    _____ good use of stress, pitch, and intonation

Oral reading:

    _____ Substitutions   _____ Mispronunciations

    _____ Additions   _____ Repetitions

    _____ Omissions   _____ Words pronounced by examiner

INSTRUCTIONAL-LEVEL GUIDE   Prepared: 3 or fewer errors   Unprepared: 6 or fewer errors   5 or more memories

GRADED PASSAGE (1C)

Assessing and Activating Background Knowledge

Here is a story about a kitten and a girl named Pat. What is it like to have a kitten?

_____ Adequate   _____ Inadequate

Motivating Statement   *Read the story to learn about the girl named Pat and the kitten.*

PAT AND THE KITTEN

Pat saw a kitten. It was on the side of the street. It was sitting under a blue car.

"Come here, little kitten," Pat said. The kitten looked up at Pat. It had big yellow eyes. Pat took her from under the car. She saw that her leg was hurt.

"I will take care of you," Pat said. She put her hand on the kitten's soft, black fur. "You can come home with me."

The kitten gave a happy *meow.*   (80 words)

Unprompted Memories

Please retell the story.

_____ Pat saw kitten

_____ on side of street/under car

_____ come here, Pat said

_____ kitten looked up

_____ big yellow eyes, black fur

_____ her leg was hurt

_____ I will take care of you

_____ Pat put hand on fur

_____ come home with me

_____ kitten meowed happily

Comprehension Questions

_____ *What did Pat see?*   (kitten)

_____ *Where was the kitten?*   (side of street)

_____ (under car)

_____ *What did Pat first say to the kitten?*   (come here, little kitten)

_____ *What did the kitten look like?*   (yellow eyes)

_____ (black fur)

_____ *What was the matter with the kitten?*   (hurt leg)

_____ *What did Pat say to the kitten when she saw it was hurt?*

(I will take care of you)

_____ *What did Pat want to do with the kitten?*   (take home)

_____ *What did the kitten do?*   (meowed happily)

Interpretive question: *Why was the kitten happy at the end of the story?*

Acceptable answer: _____ Yes   _____ No

Memories: _____ Unprompted + _____ Prompted = _____ Total

Organized retelling: _____ Yes   _____ No

Oral reading inaccuracies changed meaning: _____ Yes   _____ No

Rate appropriate: _____ Yes   _____ No   Fluency appropriate: _____ Yes   _____ No

_____ reads word by word   _____ reads in phrases   _____ good use of punctuation

_____ good use of stress, pitch, and intonation

Oral reading:

_____ Substitutions   _____ Mispronunciations

_____ Additions   _____ Repetitions

_____ Omissions   _____ Words pronounced by examiner

INSTRUCTIONAL-LEVEL GUIDE   **Prepared: 4 or fewer errors**   **Unprepared: 8 or fewer errors**   **6 or more memories**

GRADED PASSAGE (1C/A)

Assessing and Activating Background Knowledge

Here is a story about a man named Tony who lived in a city. What do you think he didn't like about the city?

_____ Adequate   _____ Inadequate

Motivating Statement   *Read the story to learn about Tony and what he did in the city.*

TONY AND THE FLOWER SHOP

Tony lived in a big city. He had a flower shop. Tony loved his flowers, for the flowers did not make any noise. Tony loved peace and quiet.

The city where Tony lived was noisy. The buses, trucks, and cars were very noisy. He did not like the noise of the city.

Without the quiet Tony found in the flower shop, he would have moved from the city. The flower shop was his only reason for staying in the city.   (80 words)

Unprompted Memories

Please retell the story.

_____ Tony lived in city

_____ owned a flower shop

_____ loved his flowers, quiet

_____ city was noisy

_____ buses, trucks, cars

_____ quiet shop

_____ would move from city

_____ flower shop was reason for staying in city

Comprehension Questions

_____ *Where did Tony live?*   (big city)

_____ *What did Tony do?*   (owned or had flower shop)

_____ *Why did Tony like his flowers?*   (they were quiet)

_____ *Why did Tony dislike the city?*   (the noise)

_____ *Why was the city noisy?*   (buses)

_____ (trucks)

_____ (cars)

_____ *What did the flower shop give Tony?*   (peace and quiet)

_____ *What was the reason for staying in the city?*

          (he liked his flower shop)

Interpretive question: *Why do you think Tony likes peace and quiet?*

          Acceptable answer: _____ Yes _____ No

Memories: _____ Unprompted + _____ Prompted = _____ Total

Organized retelling: _____ Yes _____ No

Oral reading inaccuracies changed meaning: _____ Yes _____ No

Rate appropriate: _____ Yes _____ No   Fluency appropriate: _____ Yes _____ No

          _____ reads word by word   _____ reads in phrases   _____ good use of punctuation

          _____ good use of stress, pitch, and intonation

Oral reading:

_____ Substitutions   _____ Mispronunciations

_____ Additions   _____ Repetitions

_____ Omissions   _____ Words pronounced by examiner

INSTRUCTIONAL-LEVEL GUIDE   Prepared: 4 or fewer errors   Unprepared: 8 or fewer errors   6 or more memories

GRADED PASSAGE (1A)

Assessing and Activating Background Knowledge

Here is a story about an old man who solved a problem. What kinds of problems do older people have?

_____ Adequate   _____ Inadequate

Motivating Statement   *Read the story to learn about some things an old man did and how he made his life easier.*

GIVE ME ROOM

I saw an old man get on the bus. He walked very slowly. He used a cane. I looked at the cane with surprise. The man had a bike horn on it. I told him I had never seen a cane with a horn. "Have you ever been to the city market?" he asked. I said that I had. "Then you know it is crowded," he said. "People did not give me room. Now I honk my horn and they move."   (81 words)

Unprompted Memories

Please retell the story.

_____ saw old man on bus

_____ walked slowly using cane

_____ surprised at horn on cane

_____ never saw a cane with horn

_____ been to market? he asked

_____ said yes

_____ it is crowded, he said

_____ people didn't give me room

_____ now honks and they move

Comprehension Questions

_____ *Who did the person see?*   (an old man)

_____ *What was the old man doing?*   (got on a bus or walking)

_____ *Describe the old man.*   (walked slow)

_____ (used a cane)

_____ *Why was the person surprised?*   (had horn on cane)

_____ *What did the person say to the old man?*   (never saw cane with horn on it)

_____ *What caused the problem for the old man?*   (crowded market)

_____ *Why did the person understand the problem at the market?* (he had been there)

_____ *Why did he use a horn?*   (to get people to move)

Interpretive question: *Why did people move when he honked?*

        Acceptable answer: _____ Yes   _____ No

Memories: _____ Unprompted + _____ Prompted = _____ Total

Organized retelling: _____ Yes   _____ No

Oral reading inaccuracies changed meaning: _____ Yes   _____ No

Rate appropriate: _____ Yes   _____ No   Fluency appropriate: _____ Yes   _____ No

        _____ reads word by word   _____ reads in phrases   _____ good use of punctuation

        _____ good use of stress, pitch, and intonation

Oral reading:

    _____ Substitutions   _____ Mispronunciations

    _____ Additions   _____ Repetitions

    _____ Omissions   _____ Words pronounced by examiner

INSTRUCTIONAL-LEVEL GUIDE   **Prepared: 4 or fewer errors   Unprepared: 8 or fewer errors   6 or more memories**

GRADED PASSAGE (2C)

Assessing and Activating Background Knowledge

Here is a story about a little frog. What do you know about frogs?

_____ Adequate   _____ Inadequate

Motivating Statement   *Read the story to learn how this little frog lived.*

THE SONG OF LITTLE FROG

Little Frog lived by a lake. He did not have many things. He only had a house to live in, a bed to sleep in, and an old pot to cook with. He had one old book that he read again and again. Still Little Frog was happy.

Near his house there were many pretty flowers. The birds sang all day. Little Frog liked to look at the pretty flowers. He liked to hear the birds sing. Little Frog wanted to sing like the birds. But when he tried to sing, all that came out was a *ribbit ribbit.*   (99 words)

Unprompted Memories

Please retell the story.

_____ Little Frog

_____ lived by a lake

_____ had a house, bed, and pot

_____ had an old book

_____ read again and again

_____ near house flowers, birds

_____ he wanted to

_____ sing like birds

_____ he tried

_____ just *ribbit ribbit*

Comprehension Questions

_____ *Where did Little Frog live?*   (by a lake)

_____ (in a house)

_____ *What did he own?*   (pot)

_____ (bed)

_____ *Why did he read the same book?*   (only had one book)

_____ *How did Little Frog feel?*   (happy)

_____ *What things were near his house?*   (flowers)

_____ (birds)

_____ *Why did he like the birds?*   (they sang)

_____ *What happened when he tried to sing?*   (ribbit ribbit)

Interpretive question: *Why was Little Frog happy with just a few things?*

      Acceptable answer: _____ Yes _____ No

Memories: _____ Unprompted + _____ Prompted = _____ Total

Organized retelling: _____ Yes _____ No

Oral reading inaccuracies changed meaning: _____ Yes _____ No

Rate appropriate: _____ Yes _____ No   Fluency appropriate: _____ Yes _____ No

      _____ reads word by word   _____ reads in phrases   _____ good use of punctuation

      _____ good use of stress, pitch, and intonation

Oral reading:

      _____ Substitutions   _____ Mispronunciations

      _____ Additions   _____ Repetitions

      _____ Omissions   _____ Words pronounced by examiner

INSTRUCTIONAL-LEVEL GUIDE   Prepared: 5 or fewer errors   Unprepared: 10 or fewer errors   6 or more memories

GRADED PASSAGE (2C/A)

Assessing and Activating Background Knowledge

Here is a story about an unusual newspaper. Why do most people read newspapers?

_____ Adequate   _____ Inadequate

Motivating Statement   *Read the story to learn how a boy helps someone.*

SAM BUYS A NEWSPAPER

Sam stopped to ask Mrs. Kay if she needed anything from the store. She was very old. Sam liked to help her. She asked him to buy her a newspaper. Sam went to the store.

The store was closed. Sam walked for a long time to another store. He asked for a newspaper. One was folded and put into his bag.

Sam gave Mrs. Kay the paper. She said, "Oh, Sam, you are so good. I have not seen a paper written in Greek for months!"

Sam was surprised, but he just said, "You're welcome, Mrs. Kay."   (97 words)

Unprompted Memories

Please retell the story.

_____ Sam going to store

_____ he stopped at Mrs. Kay's

_____ if she needed anything

_____ Mrs. Kay is old

_____ Sam likes to help

_____ she needed paper

_____ store was closed

_____ walked a long way to another store

_____ paper folded and put into bag

_____ gave paper to Mrs. Kay

_____ she said Sam was good

_____ she hadn't seen Greek paper
      in long time

_____ Sam surprised, said you're welcome

Comprehension Questions

_____ *Where did Sam go?*   (store or Mrs. Kay's)

_____ *What did Sam ask Mrs. Kay?*   (if she needed anything)

_____ *Why did Sam stop at Mrs. Kay's?*   (he wanted to help)

_____ *Why did he like to help Mrs. Kay?*   (she's very old or
      she needed help)

_____ *What did Mrs. Kay need at the store?*   (a newspaper)

_____ *Why did Sam walk a long way?*   (first store was closed)

_____ *Where did he finally get what he needed?*   (another store)

_____ *What did Sam buy at the store?*   (newspaper)

_____ *What did Mrs. Kay say?*   (she hadn't seen a Greek newspaper
      or Sam was good)

_____ *What did Sam say to Mrs. Kay?*   (you're welcome)

Interpretive question: *Why was Sam surprised?*

    Acceptable answer: _____ Yes   _____ No

Memories: _____ Unprompted + _____ Prompted = _____ Total

Organized retelling: _____ Yes   _____ No

Oral reading inaccuracies changed meaning: _____ Yes   _____ No

Rate appropriate: _____ Yes   _____ No   Fluency appropriate: _____ Yes   _____ No

    _____ reads word by word   _____ reads in phrases   _____ good use of punctuation

    _____ good use of stress, pitch, and intonation

Oral reading:

    _____ Substitutions   _____ Mispronunciations

    _____ Additions   _____ Repetitions

    _____ Omissions   _____ Words pronounced by examiner

INSTRUCTIONAL-LEVEL GUIDE   Prepared: 5 or fewer errors   Unprepared: 9 or fewer errors   6 or more memories

Using Graded Reader's Passages

GRADED PASSAGE (2A)

Assessing and Activating Background Knowledge

Here is a story about Linda, who works in a diner. What is a diner?

_____ Adequate   _____ Inadequate

Motivating Statement   *Read the story to learn what Linda does to improve or make her life better.*

LINDA AT THE DINER

Linda has a part-time job in a diner. She works in the morning from six until ten. The diner is busy at breakfast time. Linda works hard, but she likes her job at the diner. She likes talking with people. Many of the same people come in every day.

At night Linda goes to school. She likes night school. She has made new friends in her classes. The teachers are very nice.

Linda wants to learn more about business. She hopes to become a manager of a diner. Then she wants to buy her own diner someday.   (98 words)

Unprompted Memories

Please retell the story.

_____ Linda has part-time job

_____ at diner from 6 A.M. until 10 A.M.

_____ diner busy at breakfast

_____ likes talking to people

_____ goes to night school

_____ likes night school

_____ made new friends

_____ teachers nice

_____ wants to study business

_____ hopes to become manager

_____ wants to buy own diner

Comprehension Questions

_____ *Where does Linda work?*   (at diner)

_____ *When does Linda work?*   (6–10 A.M.)

_____ *When is the diner busy?*   (breakfast time)

_____ *Why does Linda like to work at the diner?*   (talk with people)

_____ *What does Linda do in the evening?*   (goes to night school)

_____ (new friends)

_____ *Why does Linda go to school?*   (learn business)

_____ *What does she want to do someday?*   (manage diner)

_____ (buy her own diner)

Interpretive question: *Why does Linda feel she should go to night school?*

       Acceptable answer: _____ Yes   _____ No

Memories: _____ Unprompted + _____ Prompted = _____ Total

Organized retelling: _____ Yes   _____ No

Oral reading inaccuracies changed meaning: _____ Yes   _____ No

Rate appropriate: _____ Yes   _____ No   Fluency appropriate: _____ Yes   _____ No

       _____ reads word by word   _____ reads in phrases   _____ good use of punctuation

       _____ good use of stress, pitch, and intonation

Oral reading:

       _____ Substitutions   _____ Mispronunciations

       _____ Additions   _____ Repetitions

       _____ Omissions   _____ Words pronounced by examiner

INSTRUCTIONAL-LEVEL GUIDE   Prepared: 5 or fewer errors   Unprepared: 10 or fewer errors   6 or more memories

GRADED PASSAGE (3C)

Assessing and Activating Background Knowledge

Here is a story about a boy named James and how he hurt himself. What is it like to have an accident and hurt yourself?

_____ Adequate   _____ Inadequate

Motivating Statement   *Read the story to learn about the accident that James had and what was done to help him.*

JAMES' CUT

It was after lunch when James cut his finger on the playground. He was bleeding and he hurt a little, too.

He went inside to find his teacher. He showed her his cut finger and asked for a Band-Aid. She looked at it and said, "Well, it's not too bad, James. I think we should wash it before we bandage it, don't you?" James did not want it washed because he thought it would sting. But he was afraid to tell Miss Smith. He just acted brave.

When it was washed and bandaged, he thanked Miss Smith. Then he rushed out to the playground to show everyone his shiny new bandage.   (111 words)

Unprompted Memories

Please retell the story.

_____ James cut finger
_____ on playground after lunch
_____ bleeding and hurt
_____ went to teacher, showed finger
_____ asked for a Band-Aid
_____ she looked and said wash first
_____ then bandage
_____ James didn't want it washed
_____ he thought it would sting
_____ acted brave when washed and bandaged
_____ said thank-you, went back to playground
_____ showed everyone his new bandage

Comprehension Questions

_____ *What happened to James?*   (cut his finger)
_____ *When did he hurt himself?*   (after lunch)
_____ *Where did the accident happen?*   (on the playground)
_____ *Where did James go when he cut his finger?*   (inside school to find teacher)
_____ *What did the teacher say?*   (they should wash it)
_____ *Why didn't James want it washed?*   (thought it would sting)
_____ *How did James act when his finger was washed?*   (brave)
_____ *What did he do after it was bandaged?*   (said thank-you)
_____ (went back to playground)
_____ *What did he show his friends?*   (new bandage)

Interpretive question: *Why didn't James want to tell Miss Smith he was afraid to have his finger washed?*
        Acceptable answer: _____ Yes _____ No
Memories: _____ Unprompted + _____ Prompted = _____ Total
Organized retelling: _____ Yes _____ No
Oral reading inaccuracies changed meaning: _____ Yes _____ No
Rate appropriate: _____ Yes _____ No   Fluency appropriate: _____ Yes _____ No
        _____ reads word by word   _____ reads in phrases   _____ good use of punctuation
        _____ good use of stress, pitch, and intonation
Oral reading:
        _____ Substitutions   _____ Mispronunciations
        _____ Additions   _____ Repetitions
        _____ Omissions   _____ Words pronounced by examiner

INSTRUCTIONAL-LEVEL GUIDE   Prepared: 6 or fewer errors   Unprepared: 11 or fewer errors   6 or more memories

GRADED PASSAGE (3C/A)

Assessing and Activating Background Knowledge
Here is a story about astronauts and deep-sea divers. What do they have in common?

_____ Adequate   _____ Inadequate

Motivating Statement   *Read the story to learn about what astronauts and deep-sea divers do.*

TODAY'S EXPLORERS

Astronauts fly far away from the earth. They explore space and the moon. Maybe, in time, they will explore other worlds, too. Deep-sea divers go to the floor of the sea. They explore places just as strange and wonderful as astronauts do.

You may have seen some beautiful fish in the ocean. If you were a diver, you could go far underwater. You could stay there long enough to see many unusual creatures. You would find things you never dreamed of.

The only way you could stay underwater for more than a short time is to use special gear. You must use the same kind of gear divers use. A large air tank lets you stay underwater for an hour.

Today, explorers go under the sea and far into space.   (130 words)

Unprompted Memories
Please retell the story.

_____ astronauts fly from earth

_____ explore moon and space, other worlds

_____ deep-sea divers go to sea floor

_____ they explore strange and wonderful places

_____ may have seen fish in ocean

_____ divers go far under water

_____ may see unusual creatures

_____ find things you never dream of

_____ stay under, use special gear

_____ kind of gear divers use

_____ air tank lets you stay under water for an hour

_____ explorers go under sea and into space

Comprehension Questions

_____ *Where do astronauts explore?*   (space and moon)

_____ *Where might they explore in future?*   (other worlds)

_____ *Where do divers explore?*   (sea floor) (ocean)

_____ *What may you have seen in the ocean?*   (beautiful fish)

_____ *What could you see if you were a diver?*   (unusual creatures or things you haven't dreamed of)

_____ *How do divers stay under water?*   (use special gear or air tank)

_____ *How long can a larger air tank let you stay under water?* (an hour)

_____ *Where do explorers go today?*   (in the ocean and into space)

Interpretive question: *Why do astronauts and deep-sea divers enjoy their jobs?*

     Acceptable answer: _____ Yes _____ No

Memories: _____ Unprompted + _____ Prompted = _____ Total

Organized retelling: _____ Yes _____ No

Oral reading inaccuracies changed meaning: _____ Yes _____ No

Rate appropriate: _____ Yes _____ No   Fluency appropriate: _____ Yes _____ No

     _____ reads word by word   _____ reads in phrases   _____ good use of punctuation

     _____ good use of stress, pitch, and intonation

Oral reading:

     _____ Substitutions   _____ Mispronunciations

     _____ Additions   _____ Repetitions

     _____ Omissions   _____ Words pronounced by examiner

INSTRUCTIONAL-LEVEL GUIDE   Prepared: 7 or fewer errors   Unprepared: 13 or fewer errors   5 or more memories

GRADED PASSAGE (3A)

Assessing and Activating Background Knowledge

Here is a story about a lucky wrong number. What usually happens if you dial the wrong number on the telephone?

_____ Adequate   _____ Inadequate

Motivating Statement   *Read the story to learn what happened as a result of a wrong number.*

THE LUCKY WRONG NUMBER

Sue and Bill were eating dinner when the telephone rang. Bill said, "I'll get it." A man asked if the washer could be delivered in the morning.

Bill said, "We did not order a washer."

The man said, "Is this the home of Pete Johnson?"

"No," Bill said, "but wait; Pete Johnson is our uncle's name, and we haven't seen him in a long time. What address do you have for him?"

The caller said, "201 Second Street."

Bill and Sue went to the address of Pete Johnson. He was their uncle. They were happy to see each other. Later Sue said, "Buying that washer was lucky."

Uncle Pete laughed, "I didn't buy a washer; I bought a TV. We just had a lucky wrong number."   (126 words)

Unprompted Memories

Please retell the story.

_____ Bill and Sue eating dinner

_____ phone rang

_____ asked about delivering washer

_____ we did not buy washer

_____ is this Pete Johnson's home

_____ no, but that is uncle's name

_____ haven't seen him for long time

_____ asked for address and went there

_____ he was uncle; glad to see one another

_____ buying washer good luck

_____ didn't buy washer, bought TV

_____ lucky wrong number

Comprehension Questions

_____ *What were Bill and Sue doing at the beginning of the story?* (eating dinner)

_____ *What happened while they were eating?*   (phone rang)

_____ *What did the caller want?*   (see if washer could be delivered)

_____ *Why was this a confusing situation?*   (they didn't order a new washer)

_____ *Where was the washer supposed to go?*   (Pete Johnson)

_____ *Who was Pete Johnson?*   (their uncle)

_____ *What did Bill and Sue ask the caller for?*   (the address of Pete Johnson)

_____ *Where did Bill and Sue go then?*   (Pete Johnson's address or home)

_____ *Why were they happy to see one another?*   (hadn't seen each other in long time)

_____ *What did their uncle buy?*   (TV)

Interpretive question: *How did the situation in the story help get relatives together?*

        Acceptable answer: _____ Yes   _____ No

Memories: _____ Unprompted + _____ Prompted = _____ Total

Organized retelling: _____ Yes   _____ No

Oral reading inaccuracies changed meaning: _____ Yes   _____ No

Rate appropriate: _____ Yes _____ No   Fluency appropriate: _____ Yes   _____ No

      _____ reads word by word   _____ reads in phrases   _____ good use of punctuation

      _____ good use of stress, pitch, and intonation

Oral reading:

      _____ Substitutions   _____ Mispronunciations

      _____ Additions   _____ Repetitions

      _____ Omissions   _____ Words pronounced by examiner

INSTRUCTIONAL-LEVEL GUIDE   Prepared: 6 or fewer errors   Unprepared: 13 or fewer errors   6 or more memories

GRADED PASSAGE (4C)

Assessing and Activating Background Knowledge

Here is a story about a little girl who is disabled. What does it mean to have a handicap?

_____ Adequate   _____ Inadequate

Motivating Statement   *Read the story to learn about the disability the little girl has and some things she does to help herself.*

CHECKERS GAME FOR KIM

Kim has an arm that does not work well. Sometimes Kim gets angry with her left arm because it doesn't do what she wants it to and accidents happen. When this happens, Kim gets mad and she calls her arm useless. Kim knows that with lots of exercise her left arm will work better and she will be able to do more things. Kim tries to exercise her arm as much as she can. Exercise is very hard work, but Kim keeps trying.

One way that Kim likes to exercise her arm is to help her dad make things in the workshop. She has fun working with her dad. They have just finished making a special checkers game. The checkers go into holes in the board. This will help Kim. The holes will keep the checkers from being knocked off the board by her arm. She enjoyed helping make the game because she loves to play checkers. Kim likes to work with her dad, and it is good exercise for her arm.   (172 words)

Unprompted Memories

Please retell the story.

_____ Kim's arm doesn't work well
_____ she gets angry
_____ because it doesn't work the way she wants
_____ Kim calls her arm useless
_____ exercise will make it better
_____ exercise is very hard, but she keeps trying
_____ one way to exercise is to help her dad in shop
_____ she has fun working with her dad
_____ they finished checkers game
_____ checkers go into holes
_____ keep from being knocked off by arm
_____ she enjoyed helping make game
_____ loves to play checkers
_____ good exercise for arm, too

Comprehension Questions

_____ *What was the matter with Kim?*   (she was disabled, had a bad arm)
_____ *What could Kim do to help her arm?*   (exercise)
_____ *How did Kim feel about exercise?*   (good or she knew it was hard, but kept trying)
_____ *What will lots of exercise do for Kim's arm?*   (make it better)
_____ *What was one way she exercised?*   (worked with her dad in workshop)
_____ *What did they just finish making?*   (a special checkers game)
_____ *How was the board made?*   (holes for checkers)
_____ *Why was the new board good for Kim?*   (she couldn't knock checkers off board)

Interpretive question: *Why do you think that Kim got angry and called her arm useless?*

     Acceptable answer: _____ Yes   _____ No
Memories: _____ Unprompted + _____ Prompted = _____ Total
Organized retelling: _____ Yes _____ No
Oral reading inaccuracies changed meaning: _____ Yes _____ No
Rate appropriate: _____ Yes _____ No   Fluency appropriate: _____ Yes _____ No
     _____ reads word by word   _____ reads in phrases   _____ good use of punctuation
     _____ good use of stress, pitch, and intonation
Oral reading:
     _____ Substitutions   _____ Mispronunciations
     _____ Additions   _____ Repetitions
     _____ Omissions   _____ Words pronounced by examiner

INSTRUCTIONAL-LEVEL GUIDE   Prepared: 3 or fewer errors   Unprepared: 9 or fewer errors   5 or more memories

GRADED PASSAGE (4C/A)

Assessing and Activating Background Knowledge

Here is a story about a little girl who was sick for a long time. How do you feel if you are sick?

_____ Adequate   _____ Inadequate

Motivating Statement   *Read the story to learn how the lives of the girl and her mother change.*

THE RECOVERY

In three small rooms lived a mother and her daughter, who was quite ill. The mother worked every day. She worked hard but could afford little more than rent, food, and clothes. Because of this, the little sick girl would stay quietly in bed at home while her mother was away.

The mother worried about her daughter. If only she had someone to talk to or something to keep her mind busy.

One morning as the mother was leaving for work, she saw a little hurt bird huddled on the windowsill. Her daughter insisted that it be brought in so she could care for it.

That evening when the mother returned, the daughter was more talkative than she had been for a while. Every evening after that, she noticed that both the girl and the bird were improved. They seemed to draw strength from each other.

Then one day the mother returned home to find the table set. Tears came to the mother's eyes when the little girl said they must celebrate, for the bird was better.   (177 words)

Unprompted Memories

Please retell the story.

_____ three small rooms
_____ lived a mother and sick girl
_____ mother worked hard every day
_____ she could afford only food, rent, and clothes
_____ mother worried about daughter
_____ needed someone to talk to
_____ keep her mind busy
_____ saw hurt bird on sill
_____ brought it in for girl to care for
_____ girl more talkative
_____ when mother came home
_____ both bird and girl improved

Comprehension Questions

_____ *Where did the mother and daughter live?*   (in three small rooms)
_____ *What was the matter with the little girl?*   (she was sick)
_____ *What did the mother do every day?*   (worked hard)
_____ *What could the mother afford?*   (food, rent, clothes—2 of 3)
_____ *What was found on the window sill?*   (a little hurt bird)
_____ *Where did the mother take the bird?*   (in the house or gave it to girl to care for)
_____ *How was the girl different when the mother came home?*   (more talkative)
_____ *What did the mother find when she came home?*   (table was set)
_____ *What did they celebrate?*   (the bird's recovery)

Interpretive question: *How did taking care of the bird help the girl?*

Acceptable answer: _____ Yes   _____ No
Memories: _____ Unprompted + _____ Prompted = _____ Total
Organized retelling: _____ Yes   _____ No
Oral reading inaccuracies changed meaning: _____ Yes   _____ No
Rate appropriate: _____ Yes   _____ No   Fluency appropriate: _____ Yes   _____ No
    _____ reads word by word   _____ reads in phrases   _____ good use of punctuation
    _____ good use of stress, pitch, and intonation
Oral reading:
    _____ Substitutions   _____ Mispronunciations
    _____ Additions   _____ Repetitions
    _____ Omissions   _____ Words pronounced by examiner

INSTRUCTIONAL-LEVEL GUIDE   Prepared: 4 or fewer errors   Unprepared: 9 or fewer errors   6 or more memories

GRADED PASSAGE (4A)

Assessing and Activating Background Knowledge

Here is a story about Alaska. What do you know about Alaska?

_____ Adequate   _____ Inadequate

Motivating Statement   *Read the story to learn about the purchase of Alaska and what that state is like.*

LAND OF MANY RICHES

In 1869, American Secretary of State William Seward did something that many people thought was foolish. He bought a huge piece of land called Alaska. He bought Alaska for only two cents an acre from a country called Russia. But many people thought the purchase was a waste of money. To them, Alaska was just a useless land of rocks, snow, and ice.

However, the following years have proved these people wrong. What was found in Alaska has made the purchase worthwhile. Much of the land in Alaska is covered by forests. The trees are cut and sold to all parts of the world. Oil has been found in Alaska.

The sea around Alaska is full of fish. Codfish, herring, crabs, and shrimp live there. They are caught and sold to the rest of the United States and the world. Alaska has been worth much more than it cost because much has been found there.   (155 words)

Unprompted Memories

Please retell the story.

_____ in 1869, Secretary of State Seward
_____ did something people thought was foolish
_____ bought the land called Alaska
_____ for two cents an acre from Russia
_____ people thought it was a waste of money
_____ Alaska useless land of ice, snow, and rock
_____ time proved them wrong
_____ purchase was worthwhile
_____ trees cover land
_____ they are cut and sold around the world
_____ oil was found in Alaska
_____ surrounding sea full of fish
_____ among these are codfish, herring, crabs, and shrimp
_____ caught and sold all over world
_____ Alaska worth more than its cost

Comprehension Questions

_____ *Who purchased Alaska?*   (Secretary of State Seward)
_____ *In what year was the purchase made?*   (1869)
_____ *What did some people think of the purchase?*
(very foolish)
_____ *How much did Alaska cost?*   (two cents an acre)
_____ *From what country was Alaska purchased?*
(Russia)
_____ *Why did people say Alaska was useless?*
(covered with snow, rocks, and ice)
_____ *What do they do with the trees?*   (cut and sell
all over United States and world)
_____ *What were found in the sea?*   (fish)
_____ *What do they do with the fish?*   (sell them all
over the world)
_____ *Why was Alaska worth more than its price?*
(all that was found or trees, oil, fish)

Interpretive question: *Why is it important for a country to have different kinds of riches (or natural resources)?*
       Acceptable answer: _____ Yes _____ No
Memories: _____ Unprompted + _____ Prompted = _____ Total
Organized retelling: _____ Yes _____ No
Oral reading inaccuracies changed meaning: _____ Yes _____ No
Rate appropriate: _____ Yes _____ No   Fluency appropriate: _____ Yes   No
       _____ reads word by word   _____ reads in phrases   _____ good use of punctuation
       _____ good use of stress, pitch, and intonation
Oral reading:
       _____ Substitutions   _____ Mispronunciations
       _____ Additions   _____ Repetitions
       _____ Omissions   _____ Words pronounced by examiner

INSTRUCTIONAL-LEVEL GUIDE   Prepared: 3 or fewer errors   Unprepared: 8 or fewer errors   6 or more memories

GRADED PASSAGE (5C)

Assessing and Activating Background Knowledge

Here is a story about a young hunter and an eagle. What do you know about eagles?

_____ Adequate   _____ Inadequate

Motivating Statement   *Read the story to learn about a boy's hunting adventure.*

WAUKEWA'S EAGLE

One morning when the boy called Waukewa was hunting along the mountainside, he found a young eagle with a broken wing. It was lying at the base of a cliff. The bird had fallen from a ledge and, being too young to fly, had fluttered down the cliff. It was hurt so severely that it was likely to die. When Waukewa saw it, he was about to drive one of his sharp arrows through its body. But then he saw that the young eagle at his feet was quivering with pain and fright. Waukewa slowly stooped over the panting eagle. The wild eyes of the wounded bird and the keen, dark eyes of the boy met. The boy's eyes grew gentler and softer as he gazed at the bird. Then the struggling of the young eagle stopped. The wild, frightened look passed out of its eyes. And the bird allowed Waukewa to pass his hand gently over its ruffled feathers. The desire to fight, to defend its life, gave way to the charm of the tenderness and pity expressed in the boy's eyes. From that moment, Waukewa and the eagle were friends.   (192 words)

Comprehension Questions

_____ *Who was Waukewa?*   (a boy)

_____ *Where did he find the eagle?*   (at the base of a cliff)

_____ *What injury did the eagle have when Waukewa found it?*   (broken wing)

_____ *How was the eagle's wing broken?*   (in a fall)

_____ *What was Waukewa going to do to the eagle when he first saw it?*   (kill it—put an arrow through its body)

_____ *How did Waukewa's eyes change as he looked at the bird?*   (grew gentler, softer, or expressed tenderness and pity)

_____ *How did the eagle's behavior change?*   (stopped quivering or stopped struggling)

Interpretive question: *Why did the eagle stop struggling?*

        Acceptable answer: _____ Yes _____ No

Memories: _____ Unprompted + _____ Prompted = _____ Total

Organized retelling: _____ Yes _____ No

Oral reading inaccuracies changed meaning: _____ Yes _____ No

Rate appropriate: _____ Yes _____ No   Fluency appropriate: _____ Yes _____ No

        _____ reads word by word   _____ reads in phrases   _____ good use of punctuation

        _____ good use of stress, pitch, and intonation

Oral reading:

        _____ Substitutions   _____ Mispronunciations

        _____ Additions   _____ Repetitions

        _____ Omissions   _____ Words pronounced by examiner

INSTRUCTIONAL-LEVEL GUIDE   Prepared: 4 or fewer errors   Unprepared: 10 or fewer errors   5 or more memories

GRADED PASSAGE (5C/A)

Assessing and Activating Background Knowledge

Here is a story about the Nile Valley. Why would building a water system be helpful to grow crops?

_____ Adequate   _____ Inadequate

Motivating Statement   *Read the story to learn about what the tribes who settled in the Nile Valley did.*

THE NILE VALLEY

The early settlers in the Nile Valley had to root out the jungle and drain the marshes. Once it was cleared, the flood-enriched soil produced good crops. The rich soil caused many tribes to come to settle in the valley. In time some of these tribes learned that more land could be farmed if there was water for the long dry season. They worked hard to build a lake in which to store the water. They dug miles of canals and ditches to distribute the water to the fields.

This was a large task, which required the work of many tribes. Out of common need, the many different tribes had one leader to plan and direct their work. Once the water system was built, the leader supervised its repair and controlled the flow of water into the canals. Through his control of the water, he became a powerful ruler.

(150 words)

Comprehension Questions

_____ *What did the early settlers of the Nile Valley have to do to the land?*   (root out jungle and drain marshes)

_____ *Why did the soil produce good crops?*   (flood-enriched)

_____ *Why did many tribes come to this region?*   (the good soil produced good crops, so they could prosper there)

_____ *What did the tribes learn would help during the dry season?*   (build something to store the water)

_____ *How was the water going to be distributed?*   (through miles of ditches and canals)

_____ *Why did so many different tribes agree to one leader?*   (they had a common need and all banded together to build the water system)

_____ *Why did this ruler become a powerful man?*   (he controlled the water)

Interpretive question: *Why did the early settlers of the Nile Valley want to farm the land?*

Acceptable answer: _____ Yes _____ No

Memories: _____ Unprompted + _____ Prompted = _____ Total

Organized retelling: _____ Yes _____ No

Oral reading inaccuracies changed meaning: _____ Yes _____ No

Rate appropriate: _____ Yes _____ No   Fluency appropriate: _____ Yes _____ No

_____ reads word by word   _____ reads in phrases   _____ good use of punctuation

_____ good use of stress, pitch, and intonation

Oral reading:

_____ Substitutions   _____ Mispronunciations

_____ Additions   _____ Repetitions

_____ Omissions   _____ Words pronounced by examiner

INSTRUCTIONAL-LEVEL GUIDE   Prepared: 3 or fewer errors   Unprepared: 8 or fewer errors   5 or more memories

GRADED PASSAGE (5A)

Assessing and Activating Background Knowledge

Here is a story about a man who needs glasses. Why is it so important to wear glasses if needed?

    ____ Adequate   ____ Inadequate

Motivating Statement   *Read the story to learn about what happened to Carlos and the effect of eyeglasses on reading.*

NOT IN THE MOOD TO READ

Have you ever heard someone say, "I used to like to read, but now I am not interested in reading"? Carlos used to say that. Then one day he found that he could not read the small print on a medicine bottle. Carlos had his eyes tested, and he was told he needed glasses. The day Carlos put them on, he stopped at a paperback bookstore and bought a sports magazine, a paperback mystery, and a newspaper. Carlos's eyes had never hurt, so he hadn't thought about needing glasses. It seemed good to be reading again. Carlos had forgotten how much he enjoyed reading.

There are many people, both children and adults, who believe they don't feel like reading or doing close work. Their vision is poor, but they do not know that they are having problems with their sight. However, there are others who know they should wear glasses but don't want to wear them. They think glasses may not be attractive. This is not necessarily true. Glasses now have such nice-looking frames that some people wear them who don't need them! In fact, lenses in their glasses are just plain window glass.   (195 words)

Comprehension Questions

____ *What do some people say about reading?*   (they used to like to read but don't read anymore)

____ *What happened to Carlos one day?*   (he couldn't read the label on a medicine bottle)

____ *After he got his glasses, what did Carlos buy?*   (a paperback mystery, a sports magazine, and a newspaper)

____ *Why did Carlos think that nothing was wrong with his eyes?*   (his eyes didn't hurt him)

____ *Why do some people probably not like to read?*   (they have problems with their eyes)

____ *Why do some people dislike glasses?*   (they think they are unattractive)

____ *Why do some people have window glasses instead of lenses?*   (they like the looks of glasses but don't need to wear them)

Interpretive question: *Why is reading a hobby enjoyed by people with good eyesight?*
    Acceptable answer: ____ Yes   ____ No

Memories: ____ Unprompted + ____ Prompted = ____ Total

Organized retelling: ____ Yes   ____ No

Oral reading inaccuracies changed meaning: ____ Yes   ____ No

Rate appropriate: ____ Yes   ____ No   Fluency appropriate: ____ Yes   ____ No
    ____ reads word by word   ____ reads in phrases   ____ good use of punctuation
    ____ good use of stress, pitch, and intonation

Oral reading:
    ____ Substitutions   ____ Mispronunciations
    ____ Additions   ____ Repetitions
    ____ Omissions   ____ Words pronounced by examiner

INSTRUCTIONAL-LEVEL GUIDE   Prepared: 4 or fewer errors   Unprepared: 10 or fewer errors   5 or more memories

GRADED PASSAGE (6C)

Assessing and Activating Background Knowledge

Here is a story about humans' first tools. What would first tools be like?

_____ Adequate   _____ Inadequate

Motivating Statement   *Read the story to learn about how early tools were made and used.*

EARLY TOOLS

Before humans discovered how to obtain and work metals, they made their tools out of wood, bone, and stone. At first they simply used the materials in their natural forms. Then they learned to alter the materials to produce tools to fit the tasks. Wood was split or shaved with sharp rocks and polished on sandstones. Pointed stones were used to bore holes in wood. Fire was also used to shape wood. After a portion of the wood was burnt, the charcoal was scraped away. This process was repeated until the desired shape was achieved.

Bone was broken into many different-sized splinters that were used as knives and needles.

For the most part, the wood and bone tools have not survived to this day. But it is still possible to find ancient stone tools.

Stone tools were shaped by two methods. They were struck with rocks or pieces of antler or shaped by applying pressure at points where a flake was likely to break off.

Many people have found arrowheads. Most of these were actually used as spear points. Only a very small stone head would be light enough to use with a bow and arrow.   (197 words)

Comprehension Questions

_____ *What did humans use to make tools before metal was discovered?*   (wood, bone, and stone)

_____ *How did they use these materials?*   (first in natural form, then they learned to alter material)

_____ *How was wood altered to produce tools?*   (split or shaved, polished, and burned)

_____ *For what was bone used?*   (knives and needles)

_____ *What two methods were used for shape stones?*   (struck with rock or antlers, pressing where a flake was likely to break off)

_____ *What were arrowheads actually used for?*   (spear points)

_____ *Why were arrowheads rarely used for arrows?*   (they were too large)

Interpretive question: *Why was the making of early tools a difficult task?*

    Acceptable answer: _____ Yes _____ No

Memories: _____ Unprompted + _____ Prompted = _____ Total

Organized retelling: _____ Yes _____ No

Oral reading inaccuracies changed meaning: _____ Yes _____ No

Rate appropriate: _____ Yes _____ No   Fluency appropriate: _____ Yes _____ No

    _____ reads word by word   _____ reads in phrases   _____ good use of punctuation

    _____ good use of stress, pitch, and intonation

Oral reading:

    _____ Substitutions   _____ Mispronunciations

    _____ Additions   _____ Repetitions

    _____ Omissions   _____ Words pronounced by examiner

INSTRUCTIONAL-LEVEL GUIDE   Prepared: 4 or fewer errors   Unprepared: 10 or fewer errors   5 or more memories

GRADED PASSAGE (6C/A)

Assessing and Activating Background Knowledge

Here is a story about the constellations. What are star constellations?

_____ Adequate _____ Inadequate

Motivating Statement *Read the story to learn more about the constellations and how they help us.*

CONSTELLATIONS

People all over the world have looked at the stars and have seen patterns that reminded them of everyday things. A group of stars that forms such a pattern is a constellation. A constellation lies within a definite region of the sky. By knowing the positions of the constellations, one can locate stars, planets, comets, and other galaxies. There are eighty-eight officially recognized constellations.

Many of the ancient names for certain constellations are still used today, though the things they were named for are no longer a part of our everyday experiences.

Almost anyone who grew up in the Northern Hemisphere can point out the Little Dipper. The Little Dipper is part of the constellation Ursa Minor, which means Little Bear.

Ursa Minor appears to circle the North Star. It is visible all year long. Some groups of stars are only visible during certain seasons of the year.

There are twelve seasonal constellations that are especially important because the sun and the moon always rise within one of their patterns. These are the constellations of the zodiac.

Constellations are used in ship and airplane navigation. Astronauts use them to help orient spacecraft.

(193 words)

Comprehension Questions

_____ *What do the patterns in the stars remind people of?* (everyday things)
_____ *What is a constellation?* (a group of stars that form a pattern)
_____ *How many constellations are there?* (88)
_____ *What can most people in the Northern Hemisphere identify?* (Little Dipper)
_____ *What does Ursa Minor mean?* (Little Bear)
_____ *What constellation appears to circle the North Star?* (Ursa Minor)
_____ *When is Ursa Minor visible?* (all year long)
_____ *What does visible mean?* (able to be seen)
_____ *How many seasonal constellations are there?* (12)
_____ *How are constellations used?* (navigation of ships and airplanes, to orient spacecraft)

Interpretive question: *Why do the constellations hold mystery for some people?*
 Acceptable answer: _____ Yes _____ No
Memories: _____ Unprompted + _____ Prompted = _____ Total
Organized retelling: _____ Yes _____ No
Oral reading inaccuracies changed meaning: _____ Yes _____ No
Rate appropriate: _____ Yes _____ No   Fluency appropriate: _____ Yes _____ No
 _____ reads word by word _____ reads in phrases _____ good use of punctuation
 _____ good use of stress, pitch, and intonation
Oral reading:
 _____ Substitutions _____ Mispronunciations
 _____ Additions _____ Repetitions
 _____ Omissions _____ Words pronounced by examiner

INSTRUCTIONAL-LEVEL GUIDE **Prepared: 4 or fewer errors** **Unprepared: 10 or fewer errors** **6 or more memories**

GRADED PASSAGE (6A)

Assessing and Activating Background Knowledge
Here is a story about driver's license requirements. Why is it necessary to have a license to drive?

_____ Adequate   _____ Inadequate

Motivating Statement   *Read the story to learn more about license requirements and important information about driving.*

DRIVER'S LICENSES

States vary in their requirements for a driver's license. Some will give a license to persons sixteen years of age, while others will not. Usually the consent of a parent or guardian is needed if an applicant is under eighteen.

Generally, people need to fulfill three important requirements to get a driver's license. Drivers have to prove skills in driving a vehicle and knowledge of rules and safety procedures. They also have to be physically capable of safe driving. For example, people who are nearsighted are often issued restricted licenses. This means that they must wear glasses or contact lenses when they drive.

Responsible people drive carefully to avoid hurting others or themselves. Most of us realize that having a driver's license suspended or revoked can be very inconvenient. This is especially true when driving is needed for daily commuting to work.

Some states have a system of points. This means that for every rule the driver does not obey, points are held against him or her. If a driver has too many points in a particular period, the license to drive will be suspended. The system seems to work because people don't want to lose their driving privileges.   (199 words)

Comprehension Questions

_____ *How do states differ in their age requirements for a driver's license?*   (some issue licenses at 16; others won't)
_____ *Whose consent is sometimes needed if the applicant is under eighteen?*   (parent or guardian)
_____ *What are the three requirements necessary to obtain a driver's license?*   (skill in driving, knowledge of rules, physically able to drive)
_____ *What is a restricted license?*   (for those who must wear glasses and so on)
_____ *Explain the point system used in some states.*   (points are counted against your license for breaking rules)
_____ *What can happen if you get too many points?*   (your license may be suspended or taken away)
_____ *Why is the system helpful?*   (keeps people thinking about their responsibility behind the wheel—people don't want to lose their licenses)
_____ *Why is having your driver's license revoked an inconvenience?*   (can't do the normal things that you would do with a license)

Interpretive question: *Why is it important to have only responsible people driving cars?*
     Acceptable answer: _____ Yes _____ No
Memories: _____ Unprompted + _____ Prompted = _____ Total
Organized retelling: _____ Yes _____ No
Oral reading inaccuracies changed meaning: _____ Yes _____ No
Rate appropriate: _____ Yes _____ No   Fluency appropriate: _____ Yes _____ No
     _____ reads word by word   _____ reads in phrases   _____ good use of punctuation
     _____ good use of stress, pitch, and intonation
Oral reading:
     _____ Substitutions   _____ Mispronunciations
     _____ Additions   _____ Repetitions
     _____ Omissions   _____ Words pronounced by examiner

INSTRUCTIONAL-LEVEL GUIDE   Prepared: 4 or fewer errors   Unprepared: 10 or fewer errors   5 or more memories

GRADED PASSAGE (7C)

Assessing and Activating Background Knowledge

Here is a story about volcanoes. Tell me what you know about volcanoes.

_____ Adequate   _____ Inadequate

Motivating Statement   *Read the story to learn how volcanoes are created and what happens to them.*

VOLCANOES

Powerful forces within the earth cause volcanoes. Scientists do not fully understand these forces, but they have developed theories on how the forces create volcanoes.

A volcano begins deep in the earth, where it is hot enough to melt rock. The molten rock is mixed with gases and floats up through the solid rock around it. Where the earth's crust is weakest, the liquid rock sometimes channels through it and explodes onto the surface in a volcanic eruption.

The melted rock is magma when it is still within the earth. Once it reaches the earth's surface, it is lava.

The lava flows out of the central channel and smaller side channels in streams or in sheets that overlap each other like waves on a beach.

The main gas released by a volcano is steam. Because the steam contains volcanic dust, it looks like smoke.

When the magma is sticky, rock fragments of various sizes are also thrown off by the explosion. The largest fragments are called bombs.

The material brought to the surface during a volcanic eruption sometimes forms a mountain around the opening of the central channel. A mountain that was formed by a volcano will have a large, bowl-like crater in its center, and it is also called a volcano.   (213 words)

Comprehension Questions

_____ *Where does a volcano begin?*   (deep in the earth)

_____ *What is molten rock?*   (rock so hot that it has melted)

_____ *How does the molten rock reach the surface?*   (channels through weak places in the earth's surface)

_____ *What is magma?*   (melted rock below earth's surface)

_____ *What is magma called when it reaches the earth's surface?*   (lava)

_____ *What is the main gas released by a volcano?*   (steam)

_____ *Why is this gas the color of smoke?*   (contains volcanic dust)

_____ *What happens when the magma is sticky?*   (rock fragments are thrown off by the explosion)

_____ *What are these fragments called?*   (bombs)

_____ *What is a crater?*   (bowl-like structure in the middle of the volcano)

Interpretive question: *Why can volcanoes be dangerous?*

     Acceptable answer: _____ Yes _____ No

Memories: _____ Unprompted + _____ Prompted = _____ Total

Organized retelling: _____ Yes _____ No

Oral reading inaccuracies changed meaning: _____ Yes _____ No

Rate appropriate: _____ Yes _____ No   Fluency appropriate: _____ Yes _____ No

     _____ reads word by word   _____ reads in phrases   _____ good use of punctuation

     _____ good use of stress, pitch, and intonation

Oral reading:

     _____ Substitutions   _____ Mispronunciations

     _____ Additions   _____ Repetitions

     _____ Omissions   _____ Words pronounced by examiner

INSTRUCTIONAL-LEVEL GUIDE   Prepared: 4 or fewer errors   Unprepared: 11 or fewer errors   6 or more memories

Using Graded Reader's Passages

GRADED PASSAGE (7C/A)

Assessing and Activating Background Knowledge

Here is a story about dinosaurs. How do people learn about dinosaurs?

_____ Adequate   _____ Inadequate

Motivating Statement   *Read the story to learn what scientists discovered about dinosaurs.*

QUESTIONS ABOUT DINOSAURS

Did dinosaurs take care of their young? We know that dinosaurs laid eggs. Ducks lay eggs, and they raise their young ducklings. But turtles lay eggs and, when the eggs hatch, the young turtles are on their own. When we think about birds, snakes, alligators, and other creatures that lay eggs, we can see that some care for their young and others do not.

Since the first dinosaur fossils were discovered, scientists have been curious about how they lived. The question about dinosaurs was answered when scientists found dinosaur footprints with the large prints on the outer circle and very small footprints on the inside. This discovery meant that the adult dinosaurs were protecting the young ones. If you have seen reports on elephants, you probably know that this is exactly what adult elephants do. They form a circle with each elephant in the herd facing outward so they can see lions or other animals approaching them. The tiny young elephants are safe inside the circle.

Scientists continue to ask questions, look for clues, and try to interpret what they find. Because dinosaurs were very different from each other in size, eating habits, and other ways, we don't know if all dinosaurs raised their young. Many questions have been answered about dinosaurs, but more questions remain.   (216 words)

Comprehension Questions

_____ *What question did scientists have about dinosaurs?*   (Did they take care of their young?)

_____ *Did dinosaurs lay eggs?*   (yes)

_____ *Do all creatures that lay eggs raise their young?*   (no)

_____ *Which egg layers raise their young?*   (ducks)

_____ *Which egg layers do not raise their young?*   (turtles)

_____ *How did the dinosaur footprints answer the scientists' question?*   (the tiny footprints of the young were inside the circle of adult footprints)

_____ *What animals alive today protect their young inside a circle?*   (elephants)

_____ *Do we know if all dinosaurs cared for their young? Why?*   (no, there were different kinds)

Interpretive question: *How do scientists get most of their information about dinosaurs?*

Acceptable answer: _____ Yes _____ No

Memories: _____ Unprompted + _____ Prompted = _____ Total

Organized retelling: _____ Yes _____ No

Oral reading inaccuracies changed meaning: _____ Yes _____ No

Rate appropriate: _____ Yes _____ No   Fluency appropriate: _____ Yes _____ No

_____ reads word by word   _____ reads in phrases   _____ good use of punctuation

_____ good use of stress, pitch, and intonation

Oral reading:

_____ Substitutions   _____ Mispronunciations

_____ Additions   _____ Repetitions

_____ Omissions   _____ Words pronounced by examiner

INSTRUCTIONAL-LEVEL GUIDE   Prepared: 4 or fewer errors   Unprepared: 11 or fewer errors   6 or more memories

Using Graded Reader's Passages

GRADED PASSAGE (7A)

Assessing and Activating Background Knowledge

Here is a story about getting a job. Why is a job application important in getting a job?

_____ Adequate   _____ Inadequate

Motivating Statement   *Read the story to learn more about the job application.*

THE JOB APPLICATION

Tina wanted a job in an office. A magazine publishing company had some openings, so Tina went to the personnel department. The receptionist gave her an application form and asked her to go into the next room and complete it. The form was only two pages long, but it had several parts. At the top of the first page, Tina had to write her name, address, and social security number. She was glad that she had put her social security card in her wallet. Next Tina was asked about her record of business experience. That part was easy too, except for the box that said, "Reason for separation." Tina was puzzled, but then she realized they were asking why she had lost her other job. She thought she could explain why she left, but Tina didn't know how she could write the reason in such a tiny box.

The last part of the application asked for names, occupations, and addresses of three references. Tina could not remember the addresses of her references. She didn't know whether to leave that part blank or come back later. Then she had a better idea. Tina used the telephone directory to find the correct addresses. Tina decided that before she applied for any more jobs, she would write down the kind of information needed on applications and take it with her.   (227 words)

Comprehension Questions

_____ *Where did Tina apply for a job?*   (at a magazine publishing company)

_____ *Where did she go when she went to the publishing company?*   (personnel office)

_____ *What did the receptionist tell Tina to do?*   (go to next room and fill out application form)

_____ *On the first page, what information did Tina have to know?*   (name, address, and social security number)

_____ *What else was she asked about?*   (record of business experience)

_____ *What does "reason for separation" mean?*   (reason for leaving her job)

_____ *Why was this a problem?*   (first she couldn't understand the question; then she couldn't explain the reason in such a small space)

_____ *What did the last part of the application ask for?*   (three references)

_____ *How did she find the addresses?*   (looked in the phone book)

_____ *What will she do from now on when she applies for a job?*   (write down information needed and take it with her)

Interpretive question: *If a box on a form is too small, what might an applicant do to provide complete information?*

Acceptable answer: _____ Yes _____ No

Memories: _____ Unprompted + _____ Prompted = _____ Total

Organized retelling: _____ Yes _____ No

Oral reading inaccuracies changed meaning: _____ Yes _____ No

Rate appropriate: _____ Yes _____ No   Fluency appropriate: _____ Yes _____ No

     _____ reads word by word   _____ reads in phrases   _____ good use of punctuation

     _____ good use of stress, pitch, and intonation

Oral reading:

     _____ Substitutions   _____ Mispronunciations

     _____ Additions   _____ Repetitions

     _____ Omissions   _____ Words pronounced by examiner

INSTRUCTIONAL-LEVEL GUIDE   Prepared: 5 or fewer errors   Unprepared: 11 or fewer errors   6 or more memories

GRADED PASSAGE (8C)

Assessing and Activating Background Knowledge

What reasons might men have to use a raft?

_____ Adequate   _____ Inadequate

Motivating Statement   *Read the story to learn about a voyage made on a raft.*

KON-TIKI

In 1947, six men set out to cross the Pacific Ocean from Peru to Polynesia—4,300 miles of open ocean—on a raft! This was the famous *Kon-Tiki* expedition, led by Thor Heyerdahl, a Norwegian archaeologist.

These men were attempting to prove that the people of Polynesia had originally come from Peru by crossing the ocean on a raft and that they had been led by a man called Kon-Tiki. Since no one would believe that it was possible to make such a voyage, these six decided to show that it was. They built a raft similar to the ancient Peruvian ones. They took no modern equipment except for a small radio. Nothing steered their craft besides the wind and current, yet they succeeded in making the crossing.

Erik Hesselberg, the only licensed sailor on board, was the navigator of the raft, which was named *Kon-Tiki*. He was also an accomplished artist. He brought along a bottle of ink. He sketched a little every day on the raft in order to have a record for his friends and family.   (179 words)

Comprehension Questions

_____ *In what year did the* Kon-Tiki *expedition take place?*   (1947)
_____ *How many miles did the trip involve?*   (4,300)
_____ *Who led the expedition?*   (Thor Heyerdahl)
_____ *What theory was the expedition trying to prove?*   (that the people of Polynesia had originally come from Peru)
_____ *What provisions did they take on the raft?*   (no modern equipment—just a radio)
_____ *Who was Erik Hesselberg?*   (the only licensed sailor on board)
_____ *What did he do every day aboard the raft?*   (sketched about the expedition)

Interpretive question: *Why would it be important to keep a diary of happenings on an expedition such as the* Kon-Tiki?
        Acceptable answer: _____ Yes _____ No
Memories: _____ Unprompted + _____ Prompted = _____ Total
Organized retelling: _____ Yes _____ No
Oral reading inaccuracies changed meaning: _____ Yes _____ No
Rate appropriate: _____ Yes _____ No   Fluency appropriate: _____ Yes _____ No
        _____ reads word by word   _____ reads in phrases   _____ good use of punctuation
        _____ good use of stress, pitch, and intonation
Oral reading:
        _____ Substitutions   _____ Mispronunciations
        _____ Additions   _____ Repetitions
        _____ Omissions   _____ Words pronounced by examiner

INSTRUCTIONAL-LEVEL GUIDE   Prepared: 4 or fewer errors   Unprepared: 9 or fewer errors   5 or more memories

GRADED PASSAGE (8C/A)

Assessing and Activating Background Knowledge

Why do people use a catalog to shop?

_____ Adequate   _____ Inadequate

Motivating Statement   *Read the story to learn more about mail-order shopping.*

A SHOPPING TRIP

Gene and Kim had been shopping for equipment for their camping trip. For several days they had been going from store to store looking for things they needed. Shopping was taking a lot of time and was very inconvenient. Their neighbor said that he had been shopping by sending for things through a mail-order catalog for years. Gene said that he had heard about mail-order shopping, but he was worried about getting their money back if something was wrong with the purchase. When the neighbor told Gene and Kim that the store offered a refund guarantee, they asked him if they could borrow his catalog.

Kim noticed that people could order merchandise three ways: They could place a telephone order, mail an order form, or use the Internet. Since the nearest store was far away and they did not have a computer, they planned to order by mail.

Gene felt that they had not completely wasted their time by looking through department stores because they could compare the catalog prices with the prices of items they had seen. They were both pleased to find that the measurements of hiking boots were given so that they would be able to tell whether they would fit.   (207 words)

Comprehension Questions

_____ *What had Kim and Gene been shopping for?*   (a camping trip)

_____ *Why didn't they like to shop?*   (takes a lot of time; inconvenient)

_____ *How had their neighbor been doing his shopping?*   (through a mail-order catalog)

_____ *What is a refund guarantee?*   (you can get your money back)

_____ *Why was Gene skeptical of using a mail-order catalog?*   (he was worried about getting his money back if they weren't satisfied)

_____ *What were the three ways that one could order from a catalog?*   (Internet, by phone, or by mail)

_____ *Which method did Gene and Kim decide to use?*   (they ordered by mail)

_____ *Why did Gene feel they had not wasted their time?*   (they could compare prices to those they had found in the catalog)

_____ *What were they pleased to find in the catalog?*   (measurements for boots were given)

_____ *Why was this important?*   (they could tell if the boots would fit)

Interpretive question: *Why is it important to take your time when you shop?*

  Acceptable answer: _____ Yes   _____ No

Memories: _____ Unprompted + _____ Prompted = _____ Total

Organized retelling: _____ Yes   _____ No

Oral reading inaccuracies changed meaning: _____ Yes _____ No

Rate appropriate: _____ Yes   _____ No   Fluency appropriate: _____ Yes _____ No

    _____ reads word by word   _____ reads in phrases   _____ good use of punctuation

    _____ good use of stress, pitch, and intonation

Oral reading:

    _____ Substitutions   _____ Mispronunciations

    _____ Additions   _____ Repetitions

    _____ Omissions   _____ Words pronounced by examiner

INSTRUCTIONAL-LEVEL GUIDE   Prepared: 4 or fewer errors   Unprepared: 11 or fewer errors   6 or more memories

GRADED PASSAGE (8A)

Assessing and Activating Background Knowledge

Here is a story about filling out a job application for a factory. What kind of information do you think was asked for?

_____ Adequate   _____ Inadequate

Motivating Statement *Read the story to learn about the job application form.*

A NEW JOB

Maria was interested in a job in a canning factory. She did not have much work experience, but her brother had a good job in the factory as a supervisor. Maria remembered that he had not had any experience when he started to work there.

At the personnel office, Maria was given an application form to fill out. There was a section that listed several physical problems such as rheumatism, dermatitis, and back trouble. Maria had not heard of some of the conditions, but she decided that if she didn't know what they were, she didn't have a problem with them.

Next, Maria had to check the times she was willing to work: day shift, second shift, or third shift. Because she was taking a class in adult education in the evening, she decided to check day shift and third shift. Maria hoped for the day shift, but she realized that, as a new employee without seniority, she would probably get the third shift.

Finally, Maria filled in the part of the form that asked about apprentice training. She had just finished a vocational training program that had given her some experience, so she was happy to fill in that part.

When Maria returned the completed form, she was told that she would be notified within two weeks about her employment with the company.   (224 words)

Comprehension Questions

_____ *Where did Maria want to work?*   (in a canning factory)
_____ *Who did she know that worked there?*   (her brother)
_____ *What might hinder Maria in getting the job?*   (no experience)
_____ *What was Maria given at the personnel office?*   (an application form)
_____ *What trouble did Maria have in filling out the form?*   (hadn't heard of some of the physical conditions)
_____ *What times did Maria say she was able to work?*   (day and third shift)
_____ *Why was she restricted in the times she could work?*   (she took an adult education class in the evening)
_____ *What experience did she have to add to her application?*   (she had just finished a vocational training program)
_____ *How long would it be before she was notified about the job?*   (within two weeks)
_____ *What is seniority?*   (length of time you have been with a company)

Interpretive question: *Why is it important to be flexible with time when applying for a new job?*
         Acceptable answer: _____ Yes _____ No
Memories: _____ Unprompted + _____ Prompted = _____ Total
Organized retelling: _____ Yes _____ No
Oral reading inaccuracies changed meaning: _____ Yes _____ No
Rate appropriate: _____ Yes _____ No   Fluency appropriate: _____ Yes _____ No
         _____ reads word by word   _____ reads in phrases   _____ good use of punctuation
         _____ good use of stress, pitch, and intonation
Oral reading:
         _____ Substitutions   _____ Mispronunciations
         _____ Additions   _____ Repetitions
         _____ Omissions   _____ Words pronounced by examiner

INSTRUCTIONAL-LEVEL GUIDE   Prepared: 5 or fewer errors   Unprepared: 11 or fewer errors   6 or more memories

Using Graded Reader's Passages

GRADED PASSAGE (9–10C)

Assessing and Activating Background Knowledge

This passage is about chemistry. Tell me anything you know about chemistry.

_____ Adequate   _____ Inadequate

Motivating Statement   *Read the story to learn about a modern discovery in chemistry.*

MODERN CHEMISTRY

One of the founders of modern chemistry was a wealthy Frenchman, Antoine Lavoisier, who lived in the late eighteenth century. Lavoisier burned different substances in a closed chamber and proved that there was no change in their weight. This showed that the basic elements remained the same even though their appearance was completely altered.

To explain this phenomenon, an English chemist, John Dalton, proposed the atomic theory in 1810. According to Dalton's theory, all matter is composed of minute building blocks, which he called atoms. The atoms of the different elements vary in size and characteristics. Though the elements themselves can and do combine to form new substances, their atoms always remain the same.

Guided by this theory, a Russian scientist, Dmitry Mendeleyev, arranged all of the known elements in a table according to their atomic weights. He showed that the elements fell naturally into certain groups with similar properties. Since many gaps appeared in the table, chemists began to search for the missing elements.

The field of science contains many examples of discoveries being shared by people from different nations. Because lack of communication can be disastrous to the growth of knowledge, most scientists are eager to compare results and learn from each other.   (205 words)

Comprehension Questions

_____ *Who was one of the founders of modern chemistry?*   (Antoine Lavoisier)

_____ *What important discovery did he make?*   (basic elements remained the same even though there was a change in appearance)

_____ *Who proposed the atomic theory?*   (John Dalton)

_____ *In what year was this theory proposed?*   (1810)

_____ *What term did he use to describe atoms?*   (building blocks)

_____ *How do atoms vary?*   (in size and characteristics)

_____ *Who arranged the elements in a table?*   (Dmitry Mendeleyev)

_____ *What did the table show?*   (elements fell naturally into certain groups)

_____ *What did chemists start searching for?*   (the missing elements)

Interpretive question: *Why is experimentation so important to a field like chemistry?*

Acceptable answer: _____ Yes   _____ No

Memories: _____ Unprompted + _____ Prompted = _____ Total

Organized retelling: _____ Yes   _____ No

Oral reading inaccuracies changed meaning: _____ Yes   _____ No

Rate appropriate: _____ Yes   _____ No   Fluency appropriate: _____ Yes   _____ No

_____ reads word by word   _____ reads in phrases   _____ good use of punctuation

_____ good use of stress, pitch, and intonation

Oral reading:

_____ Substitutions   _____ Mispronunciations

_____ Additions   _____ Repetitions

_____ Omissions   _____ Words pronounced by examiner

INSTRUCTIONAL-LEVEL GUIDE   Prepared: 4 or fewer errors   Unprepared: 10 or fewer errors   6 or more memories

GRADED PASSAGE (9–10C/A)

Assessing and Activating Background Knowledge

This passage is about translating one language into another. What are some problems in translating?

_____ Adequate   _____ Inadequate

Motivating Statement   *Read the story to learn more about translating.*

A FAILURE TO COMMUNICATE

When two people speak the same first language, they occasionally misunderstand each other. Imagine the difficulties that interpreters have when they must first understand what the speaker of one language has said and then translate the message into another language.

Translators are challenged when the speaker makes a reference to an event or story character that is not known to listeners from another country. A speaker may refer to someone as a "Cinderella," meaning that a person was once poor and is now wealthy, but if the listeners do not know the story, the meaning is lost.

Translating quickly, while the first person is speaking, is especially difficult. Yet, simultaneous translation is used today in about 85% of all international meetings. Not only are translators working with the United Nations, but they are employed for business, scientific, and educational meetings as well.

Computers are being programmed to translate languages. Although computers have great potential for speedy translations, they have some of the same problems that human translators have. In an early attempt to translate English into Russian, a computer translated "out of sight, out of mind" as "invisible idiot."

In our global society, we need to work hard to understand each other and keep a sense of humor.   (208 words)

Comprehension Questions

_____ *What does a translator do?*   (take a message from one language and give it to someone in another language)

_____ *What kinds of challenges do translators have?*   (translating a reference to events or stories unknown to the listeners; translating quickly or simultaneously)

_____ *What is meant by referring to someone as "Cinderella"?*   (someone who was poor and is now wealthy)

_____ *Where are translators employed?*   (United Nations; business, scientific, educational meetings)

_____ *What percentage of international meetings use translators?*   (85%)

_____ *What problem did a computer have in translating?*   (gave literal translation for a proverb; "out of sight, out of mind" translated as "invisible idiot")

_____ *What does our global society require?*   (work to understand each other and have a sense of humor)

Interpretive question: *Why do people who speak the same language have trouble understanding each other sometimes?*

     Acceptable answer: _____ Yes   _____ No

Memories: _____ Unprompted + _____ Prompted = _____ Total

Organized retelling: _____ Yes   _____ No

Oral reading inaccuracies changed meaning: _____ Yes   _____ No

Rate appropriate: _____ Yes _____ No   Fluency appropriate: _____ Yes _____ No

     _____ reads word by word   _____ reads in phrases   _____ good use of punctuation

     _____ good use of stress, pitch, and intonation

Oral reading:

     _____ Substitutions   _____ Mispronunciations

     _____ Additions   _____ Repetitions

     _____ Omissions   _____ Words pronounced by examiner

INSTRUCTIONAL-LEVEL GUIDE   Prepared: 4 or fewer errors   Unprepared: 11 or fewer errors   6 or more memories

GRADED PASSAGE (9–10A)

Assessing and Activating Background Knowledge

This passage is about a voter drive. Why is a voter drive important before an election?

_____ Adequate   _____ Inadequate

Motivating Statement   *Read the story to learn more about how a voter drive helps with registration.*

VOTER DRIVE

Soon after Jim moved to Plainfield, he received a telephone call from a person who asked if he was registered to vote in the coming election. Jim said that he hadn't thought about it. The caller said she was a member of a local organization that was sponsoring a voter drive. She didn't represent any particular political party but only wanted to encourage people to register and to vote.

Since registration terms and procedures differ from one part of the country to another, the people working in the voter drive offered to explain the local procedures and tell people where they could register.

The caller explained that after Jim registered, he would be mailed a sample ballot for each election. The ballot would contain the names of the candidates and the measures to be voted on.

Jim asked some questions and then thanked the caller for giving him information about voter registration.

Frequently people say that they don't bother to vote because one vote is not significant. Jim read that a presidential election, referred to as the Revolution of 1800, resulted in Burr and Jefferson having the same number of votes. Jim appreciated being reminded about voter registration when he recalled that important tie. (204 words)

Comprehension Questions

_____ *From whom did Jim receive a phone call?*   (a person from a local organization)

_____ *Why was she calling?*   (she was encouraging people to vote and register)

_____ *What did the caller want Jim to do?*   (register to vote)

_____ *What services was she providing?*   (explaining the local procedures and telling people where to vote)

_____ *After he registers, what will Jim receive in the mail?*   (sample ballot)

_____ *Why would that information be helpful?*   (the ballot would contain the names of candidates and measures to be voted on; one could read and study to know the candidates and issues by the election)

_____ *How does voting differ from one part of the country to another?*   (procedures and registration forms)

_____ *Why did Jim know one vote could be important?*   (remembered Burr-Jefferson tie)

Interpretive question: *Why is it important to inform yourself about the candidates and issues before you vote?*

Acceptable answer: _____ Yes _____ No

Memories: _____ Unprompted + _____ Prompted = _____ Total

Organized retelling: _____ Yes _____ No

Oral reading inaccuracies changed meaning: _____ Yes _____ No

Rate appropriate: _____ Yes _____ No   Fluency appropriate: _____ Yes _____ No

_____ reads word by word   _____ reads in phrases   _____ good use of punctuation

_____ good use of stress, pitch, and intonation

Oral reading:

_____ Substitutions   _____ Mispronunciations

_____ Additions   _____ Repetitions

_____ Omissions   _____ Words pronounced by examiner

INSTRUCTIONAL-LEVEL GUIDE   Prepared: 4 or fewer errors   Unprepared: 10 or fewer errors   5 or more memories

GRADED PASSAGE (11–12C)

Assessing and Activating Background Knowledge

Tell me about any of your favorite kinds of paintings.

_____ Adequate   _____ Inadequate

Motivating Statement   *Read the story to learn more about Impressionist art.*

IMPRESSIONISTS

Many schools of modern art have arisen, but we have space to describe only a few. The earliest group, the Impressionists, sought to capture on canvas the impression a person gets when he looks at a scene casually. They therefore merely sketched in the main features in bold brushstrokes, allowing the observer's mind to fill in the details. Similarly, they did not mix pigments on a palette in the traditional style. Instead, they used dabs of the basic colors that the viewer's eye blends to form the desired shades. Examined at close range, the Impressionists' paintings seem a blotch of colors and forms. But when the viewer steps back, they suddenly seem to come alive.

The Impressionists' work, unlike more conventional paintings, generally appeared rather flat. The founder of the post-Impressionist school, Paul Cézanne, experimented for years to remedy this weakness. He finally succeeded, by distorting the shapes of objects and using thick layers of carefully blended colors, in creating on canvas the illusion of solidity and depth.

While one may prefer a particular school of painting, an attempt should be made to understand several approaches to visual interpretations and expressions. The rewards are several: a fresh perspective, an understanding of others, and an enrichment of the aesthetic senses.   (209 words)

Comprehension Questions

_____ *What did the Impressionists try to capture on canvas?*   (what a person sees when looking casually at a scene)
_____ *What filled in the details of a painting?*   (the observer's mind)
_____ *What is the traditional style of mixing pigments?*   (using a palette)
_____ *What do Impressionist paintings resemble at close range?*   (a blotch of colors)
_____ *Who was the founder of the post-Impressionist school?*   (Paul Cézanne)
_____ *What was the weakness of Impressionistic work?*   (it appeared flat)
_____ *How did Cézanne succeed in remedying this weakness?*   (distorting shapes, using thick layers of colors)

Interpretive question: *Why is appreciating art a matter of opinion and taste?*
    Acceptable answer: _____ Yes _____ No
Memories: _____ Unprompted + _____ Prompted = _____ Total
Organized retelling: _____ Yes _____ No
Oral reading inaccuracies changed meaning: _____ Yes _____ No
Rate appropriate: _____ Yes _____ No   Fluency appropriate: _____ Yes _____ No
    _____ reads word by word   _____ reads in phrases   _____ good use of punctuation
    _____ good use of stress, pitch, and intonation
Oral reading:
    _____ Substitutions   _____ Mispronunciations
    _____ Additions   _____ Repetitions
    _____ Omissions   _____ Words pronounced by examiner

INSTRUCTIONAL-LEVEL GUIDE   Prepared: 4 or fewer errors   Unprepared: 10 or fewer errors   5 or more memories

GRADED PASSAGE (11–12C/A)

Assessing and Activating Background Knowledge

This passage is about global warfare. What does global warfare mean?

_____ Adequate   _____ Inadequate

Motivating Statement   *Read the story to learn about how global warfare has affected our country.*

GLOBAL WARFARE

Soon after it reached the White House, news of the attack on Pearl Harbor was broadcast to the American people. Many will never forget hearing newscasters breaking in on symphony concerts, football games, and children's programs to tell of the awful event. The next day the president asked Congress to accept the "state of war" that Japan's "unprovoked and dastardly attack" had thrust upon the United States; Congress accepted the challenge without dissent.

Although a brilliant military feat, the attack on Pearl Harbor eventually proved to be a colossal blunder on the part of the Japanese. To be sure, it cleared the way for an easy conquest of the Philippines and the East Indies by crippling the American naval forces in the Pacific. But the unprovoked attack united the American people as almost nothing else could have done. In their anger they forgot the bitter partisan quarrels over foreign policies and thought only how to best win a war that no one had wanted.

Subsequent analysis of the political and economic policies that contributed to the outbreak of war revealed that the events that culminated in the great war in the Pacific were the result of many factors.

After hostilities ended, both countries worked toward a harmonious relationship.

When World War II ended, representatives from many nations worked through the United Nations to develop mechanisms for avoiding the recurrence of another nightmare of violence, death, and destruction. Yet wars have continued to occur. The fighting in Southeast Asia and in the Middle East has horrified people who hoped never to see more bloodshed. Nations struggle against nations for economic, political, and cultural reasons. Resolution of complex problems is slow; yet it must come. Another global conflict, with or without the nuclear holocaust, must be avoided.   (295 words)

Comprehension Questions

_____ *How did the president describe the attack?*   (unprovoked and dastardly)

_____ *How did Congress react to the actions of Japan?*   (declared war immediately)

_____ *Why was this attack considered a "colossal blunder"?*   (it united the American people)

_____ *Why was the attack a "brilliant military feat"?*   (cleared the way for an easy conquest of the Philippines and East Indies)

_____ *Which American forces were crippled?*   (naval)

_____ *What does the word* partisan *mean?*   (taking one side)

_____ *What had the American people been quarreling about?*   (foreign policies)

_____ *What kinds of factors contributed to the cause of the war?*   (political and economic)

Interpretive question: *Why are there partisan quarrels over foreign policy?*

    Acceptable answer: _____ Yes _____ No

Memories: _____ Unprompted + _____ Prompted = _____ Total   Organized retelling: _____ Yes _____ No

Oral reading inaccuracies changed meaning: _____ Yes _____ No

Rate appropriate: _____ Yes _____ No   Fluency appropriate: _____ Yes _____ No

    _____ reads word by word   _____ reads in phrases   _____ good use of punctuation

    _____ good use of stress, pitch, and intonation

Oral reading:

    _____ Substitutions   _____ Mispronunciations

    _____ Additions   _____ Repetitions

    _____ Omissions   _____ Words pronounced by examiner

INSTRUCTIONAL-LEVEL GUIDE   Prepared: 6 or fewer errors   Unprepared: 15 or fewer errors   5 or more memories

GRADED PASSAGE (11–12A)

Assessing and Activating Background Knowledge

This passage is about people's rights. What are some rights you think workers should have?

_____ Adequate   _____ Inadequate

Motivating Statement   *Read the story to learn about how laws to protect these rights came about and why they are important.*

IMPROVEMENT FOR WORKERS

When states first passed laws regulating labor conditions, they ran into a serious difficulty. Employers challenged the laws, claiming that they interfered with a worker's freedom to work on whatever terms he chose. In 1908, a case came before the Supreme Court in which the new progressive point of view on this kind of legislation was first expressed. An Oregon law protecting women workers was called a violation of the due process clause of the Fourteenth Amendment. The lawyer defending the state of Oregon produced pages and pages of evidence to reveal how the health of women would be jeopardized unless they were protected from employers who forced them to endure long hours and paid them a meager wage. The health of women, it was argued, in the long run would affect the welfare of the nation. The Supreme Court declared that the Oregon law was constitutional.

This case was by no means the last time the Fourteenth Amendment was employed in an attempt to block reform legislation. But the decision in favor of Oregon did encourage many states to pass laws protecting labor, and the courts upheld several of them.

During periods of economic stress, pressure is often brought to bear on legislators to repeal laws that protect employees. One argument frequently heard is that by paying wages below the minimum standard, employers can afford to hire more people, thereby decreasing unemployment. Those representing workers are quick to point out that there is no guarantee that employers would expand their hiring and that improving the economy is a better alternative than offering starvation wages. A high standard of living and good working conditions are not easily surrendered.   (278 words)

Comprehension Questions

_____ *Who challenged the states who were trying to regulate labor conditions?*   (the employers)
_____ *Why were the employers challenging these laws?*   (they claimed they interfered with a worker's freedom)
_____ *In what year did a test case come before the Supreme Court?*   (1908)
_____ *Why was the Oregon law challenged?*   (called a violation of due process clause of Fourteenth Amendment)
_____ *What unfair practices were employers charged with?*   (forced women to work long hours for little pay)
_____ *What was the basis of the lawyer's case who was defending Oregon?*   (health of women hurt; this could affect nation)
_____ *Who won the case?*   (Oregon)
_____ *How did this decision affect other states?*   (they passed laws to protect labor also)

Interpretive question: *Why is it important to have good labor conditions?*
          Acceptable answer: _____ Yes _____ No
Memories: _____ Unprompted + _____ Prompted = _____ Total
Organized retelling: _____ Yes _____ No
Oral reading inaccuracies changed meaning: _____ Yes _____ No
Rate appropriate: _____ Yes _____ No   Fluency appropriate: _____ Yes _____ No
          _____ reads word by word   _____ reads in phrases   _____ good use of punctuation
          _____ good use of stress, pitch, and intonation
Oral reading:
          _____ Substitutions   _____ Mispronunciations
          _____ Additions   _____ Repetitions
          _____ Omissions   _____ Words pronounced by examiner

INSTRUCTIONAL-LEVEL GUIDE   Prepared: 6 or fewer errors   Unprepared: 14 or fewer errors   5 or more memories

PHONEMIC AWARENESS

Phonemic awareness is the understanding that spoken language consists of a sequence of phonemes. Two of the easier phonemic awareness tasks are rhyme recognition and initial phoneme recognition.

Rhyme Recognition

The term *rhyme* is not used when speaking to the child as it might introduce new vocabulary that is not needed for the task.

Directions: Say, *"Some words end the same way. Listen to these words: hat, cat, fat, sat, bat. These words all end in at. Some words do not end the same way. Listen to these words: tag, mop, car. These words do not end the same way."*

"Here are two words: big, pig. Do they end the same way?" (If the student does not give the correct response, repeat the words. Explain they both end in *ig*.)

"Here are two more words: top, bag. Do they end the same way?" (If the student gives the correct response, continue. If not, discontinue testing.)

Test items: Say, *"Good, let's do some more. I will say words and you say yes if they end the same and no if they do not end the same."* (Indicate a + or − in each space. Discontinue if the student misses three consecutive items.)

fish, dish _____	king, ring _____
cake, dog _____	bed, top _____
day, pay _____	kite, see _____
ball, tall _____	car, fed _____

Initial Phoneme Recognition

In this task, students must isolate the first phoneme in a one-syllable word (onset and rime). Continuant sounds begin the words.

Directions: Say, *"Listen to the sound at the beginning of sun. Sun starts with sssssss. What is the sound at the beginning of sun?"* If the student's answer is correct, continue; if not, repeat the directions. Next say, *"I will say a word and you tell me the beginning sound. t-en."* (Slightly emphasize the first sound without distortion.) *"What sound do you hear at the beginning?"* (If the reply is correct, continue with testing. If not, give one more, *m-an*. Discontinue if the student is unable to give a correct reply.)

Test items: Say, *"Good, let's do a few more. I will say a word and you say the sound at the beginning of the word."* (Indicate a + or − in each space. Discontinue if the student misses three items.)

fun _____	light _____	ride _____	van _____
show _____	make _____	zip _____	see _____

PHONEMIC MANIPULATION

The reader's ability to both *blend* sounds together to produce a word and *segment* a word into phonemes (sounds) involves metalinguistic skills that contribute to decoding.

Blending

Blending includes responding to a sequence of isolated speech sounds by recognizing the phonemes and pronouncing the word they constitute.

When testing the child's ability to blend, do not show the child the written material. The child hears the individual sounds and then tries to blend them together. Use the Blending test on p. 80.

Directions: Say, *"I am going to say some sounds that when put together make up a whole word. Listen to the individual sounds and then tell me the word the sounds would make when put together. Let's do one together."* Write the student's response.

Sample: *"D/I/SH makes what word?"* (dish)

Say, *"Now let's do a few more."*

Segmenting

Segmenting requires the child to discriminate the phonemes within a word and pronounce them in the correct sequence.

The child sees no written material. This skill is the reverse of blending; the child hears the word and then pronounces the phonemes or syllables separately. Use the Segmentation test on p. 80.

Directions: Say, *"I am going to say a word; then you say the sounds or word parts that make up that word. Let's do one together. In the word* dog, *the word parts are D/O/G/. Let's do a few more. I'll give you the word, and you give me the word parts."* Write the sounds the student says.

Interpretation: As children and adults learn to read and write, they usually attend to the first phoneme in a word, then the last phoneme, and finally the middle sounds (see Table 2 on p. 105). Compare the student responses here with the test results of the Hearing Letter Names in the Words test, the Spelling tests, and the Auditory Discrimination test.

Student's name _____   Date _____

BLENDING

	Word Parts	Word	Response
1.	F / EE / D	feed	_____
2.	M / A / N	man	_____
3.	D / AY	day	_____
4.	S / PI / DER	spider	_____
5.	PO / TA / TO	potato	_____

SEGMENTATION

	Word	Word Parts	Response
1.	cat	C / A / T	_____
2.	bed	B / E / D	_____
3.	soap	S / OA / P	_____
4.	time	T / I / M / E	_____
5.	face	F / A / CE	_____

Phonemic Awareness

LETTER KNOWLEDGE

Letter knowledge is divided into the areas of recognition, identification, and reproduction. A student is able to recognize a letter when, from a given list, he or she can select one that has been named by the examiner. This task is easier than letter identification, which requires the student to name the letter. If a student can identify the letters, then it is unnecessary to administer the Letter Recognition test, since it is a prerequisite skill. However, for instructional purposes, it is helpful to ascertain if the student recognizes any unidentified letters. Of the three areas, letter reproduction is the most difficult. Students may show strengths and needs in all three areas depending on the given letters. For example, an individual may be able to reproduce certain letters but only recognize or identify others. Learners ready to use a letter-name strategy in beginning word recognition may demonstrate their abilities with the Hearing Letter Names test and by their spelling.

Some children and adults who can read are unable to recite or write the alphabet in order. This ability may need to be checked.

Student's name _____   Date _____

Letter Recognition: The examiner says a letter and the student points to that letter. This is a prerequisite skill to letter identification and would only be given if the student were unable to identify the letter.

Directions: Say, *"When I name a letter, point to it."* Record all letters not known. Record all letters called in error. Look for confusion of letters: *m/n, u/n, p/b,* and *d/q.*

Letter Identification: The examiner points to a letter and the student says its name.

Directions: Say, *"Name these letters in line one, two. . . . "* Record all letters not known. Record all letters called in error. Look for confusion of letters: *m/n, u/n, p/b,* and *d/q.*

Letter Writing: The student is required to write either capital or lowercase letters of the alphabet.

Directions: Say, *"When I name a letter, write it on the paper."* Record all letters not known. Record all letters called in error. Indicate letters recognized (R), identified (I), and written (W).

ANSWER SHEET—LETTER INDENTIFICATION

Uppercase	*Known*	*Not Known*	*Lowercase*	*Known*	*Not Known*
B	____	____	m	____	____
C	____	____	y	____	____
D	____	____	n	____	____
S	____	____	l	____	____
A	____	____	r	____	____
I	____	____	o	____	____
F	____	____	t	____	____
E	____	____	p	____	____
M	____	____	z	____	____
L	____	____	v	____	____
P	____	____	k	____	____
T	____	____	i	____	____
R	____	____	a	____	____
Z	____	____	j	____	____
J	____	____	u	____	____
W	____	____	g	____	____
X	____	____	w	____	____
G	____	____	b	____	____
U	____	____	c	____	____
H	____	____	s	____	____
Q	____	____	h	____	____
K	____	____	d	____	____
N	____	____	f	____	____
Y	____	____	x	____	____
V	____	____	q	____	____
O	____	____	e	____	____

Able to recite alphabet: _____ *Yes* _____ *No*

Comments: _____

Phonemic Awareness

LETTER KNOWLEDGE

Uppercase

B C D S A I F E M L P T R

Z J W X G U H Q K N Y V O

Lowercase

m y n l r o t p z v k i a

j u g w b c s h d f x q e

HEARING LETTER NAMES IN WORDS

Those students who know the names of letters can be tested for the ability to hear letter names in words to assess a basic area of phonemic discrimination and segmentation useful in beginning reading.

Directions: Say, *"Listen to this word to see if you can hear letter names in words. Zebra. Say Zebra. What is the first letter heard in zebra?"* Give the following list of words in the same way.

Interpretation: Correct identification of at least eight letter names indicates ability to use letter names as a clue to word recognition. Students with this ability should be able to use the letter-name strategy in spelling.

1. open
2. beach
3. acorn
4. Jason
5. X-ray
6. peek
7. ice
8. deep
9. Kate
10. unicorn
11. team
12. each

HEARING LETTER NAMES IN WORDS

____ o	1.	open
____ b	2.	beach
____ a	3.	acorn
____ j	4.	Jason
____ x	5.	X-ray
____ p	6.	peek
____ i	7.	ice
____ d	8.	deep
____ k	9.	Kate
____ u	10.	unicorn
____ t	11.	team
____ e	12.	each

Phonemic Awareness

PHONICS AND STRUCTURAL ANALYSIS TESTS

CONTENTS OF THE TEST

Phonics	*Structural Analysis*
1. Initial Single Consonants	8. Inflectional Suffixes
2. Consonant Blends	9. Derivational Suffixes
3. Consonant Digraphs	10. Prefixes
4. Short-Vowel Sounds	11. Compound Words
5. Long-Vowel Sounds	
6. Vowel Digraphs	
7. Reversals	

Phonics

Information about a student's knowledge of sound-symbol association, ability to blend sounds, and knowledge of structural analysis can be obtained by administering a phonics test and analysis. The subtests in this section have been designed to determine if students know grapheme–phoneme correspondence of phonetically regular elements. Nonsense words are used to ensure that the student is not simply pronouncing words by sight. The results of this test should be compared with the student's ability to read words in context so that a qualitative analysis can be made with regard to the student's application of his or her graphemic, syntactic, and semantic knowledge.

Directions: Select only those subtests that appear to be appropriate. For example, a student who is able to read second-grade-level passages probably should not be given the subtest on consonant sounds, and a student whose highest instructional level is first grade should not be given the syllabication subtest, and so forth.

Introduce each test by reading the directions on the subtest page. Mark responses on the examiner's copy accompanying each subtest. Record student's responses by putting a line through those that are correct and writing incorrect responses above the missed elements. Circle elements not attempted. The Testing Record on p. 102 is helpful for summarization purposes.

Interpretation: Most readers apply their background of experiences and knowledge of language so that they make use of context to predict the content words in a passage. Generally, the first one or two letters of a word, along with syntactic and semantic context, are used in word recognition. When necessary, the reader resorts to an analysis of the entire word and confirms his or her results with the context. One purpose of the Phonics and Word Analysis test is to learn whether the reader has the knowledge and ability to analyze words not immediately recognized. A record can be kept of sound-symbol associations that have not been acquired, ability to blend sounds, and structural analysis abilities so that sufficient assistance can be given in these areas to enable the reader to recognize words in context. *Caution:* Some readers have great difficulty in phonetic analysis and should not be drilled in this skill. Other readers will be overly analytic in their application of phonetic and structural analysis. They will need to learn to read for meaning. These situations indicate the need for the diagnostician to put word analysis in proper perspective.

Student's name _____   Date _____

PHONICS TEST

Initial Single Consonants, Consonant Blends, and Consonant Digraphs

Directions: Say, *"Look at the two letters in the middle (shaded) column. OP is pronounced /op/. Name the letter(s) in the first column, pronounce the* op *in the middle column, and then say the nonsense word in the third column by adding the first letter(s) to the middle word."*

If necessary, tell the student the *op* sound, because the purpose in giving these subtests is to determine knowledge of the initial letter(s). The student should not have difficulty blending the initial sound with the op. Make certain the student can pronounce *op* before the test begins. When the student can identify the sound of /op/, continue with the test.

Record all responses on the answer sheet (below). Indicate any incorrect sounds substituted by the student.

Consonants, blends, and digraphs are usually introduced in the first and second grades.

ANSWER SHEET

Initial Single Consonants

1. b	7. j	13. r
2. c	8. k	14. s
3. d	9. l	15. t
4. f	10. m	16. v
5. g	11. n	17. w
6. h	12. p	18. z

Consonant Blends

1. bl	9. gr	17. sp
2. br	10. pl	18. st
3. cl	11. pr	19. sw
4. cr	12. sc	20. tr
5. dr	13. sk	21. tw
6. fr	14. sl	22. scr
7. fl	15. sm	23. str
8. gl	16. sn	

Consonant Digraphs

1. sh
2. ch
3. ph
4. th
5. wh

Phonics and Structural Analysis

PHONICS TEST
Initial Single Consonants
op

1. b	op	bop		10. m	op	mop
2. c	op	cop		11. n	op	nop
3. d	op	dop		12. p	op	pop
4. f	op	fop		13. r	op	rop
5. g	op	gop		14. s	op	sop
6. h	op	hop		15. t	op	top
7. j	op	jop		16. v	op	vop
8. k	op	kop		17. w	op	wop
9. l	op	lop		18. z	op	zop

PHONICS TEST
Consonant Blends
op

1. bl	op	blop		12. sc	op	scop
2. br	op	brop		13. sk	op	skop
3. cl	op	clop		14. sl	op	slop
4. cr	op	crop		15. sm	op	smop
5. dr	op	drop		16. sn	op	snop
6. fr	op	frop		17. sp	op	spop
7. fl	op	flop		18. st	op	stop
8. gl	op	glop		19. sw	op	swop
9. gr	op	grop		20. tr	op	trop
10. pl	op	plop		21. tw	op	twop
11. pr	op	prop		22. scr	op	scrop
				23. str	op	strop

PHONICS TEST
Consonant Digraphs
op

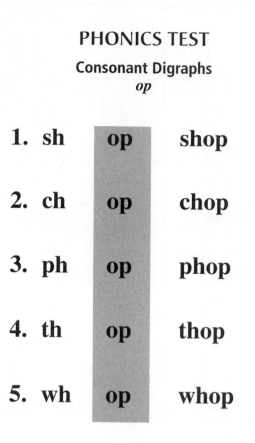

1. sh   **op**   shop

2. ch   **op**   chop

3. ph   **op**   phop

4. th   **op**   thop

5. wh   **op**   whop

Student's name _____   Date _____

Short Vowels, Long Vowels, and Vowel Digraphs

Directions: Nonsense words are used when testing for knowledge of grapheme–phoneme relationships to ensure the word is not known by sight. Say, *"Look at the letter(s) in the middle column; then pronounce the nonsense or silly word beside it."*

     Record the answer on the answer sheet (below) by indicating incorrect responses.

     Short- and long-vowel sounds are usually introduced in first grade, and vowel digraphs in the second and third grades.

ANSWER SHEET

Short Vowels	*Long Vowel—Silent* e *Ending*
1. a	6. i
2. i	7. o
3. e	8. e
4. o	9. u
5. u	10. a

Long Vowels—Double Vowel Combinations

11. oa
12. ea
13. ai
14. ee

Vowel Digraphs

15. oo (as in *loose, food*)	20. oi (as in *oil*)
16. oo (as in *cook, stood*)	21. oy (as in *boy*)
17. ew (as in *few, stew*)	22. ou (as in *out*)
18. au (as in *author*)	23. ow (as in *cow*)
19. aw (as in *straw*)	24. ow (as in *mow*)

Phonics and Structural Analysis

PHONICS TEST

Short-Vowel Sounds

1. a   fap
2. i   fip
3. e   fep
4. o   fop
5. u   fup

Long Vowels—Silent e Ending

6. i   fite
7. o   fote
8. e   fete
9. u   fute
10. a   fate

Long Vowels—Double Vowel Combinations

11. oa   oam
12. ea   eam
13. ai   aim
14. ee   eem

PHONICS TEST
Vowel Digraphs

15. oo—tood

16. oo—sook

17. ew—tew

    lew

18. au—aut

    aup

19. aw—awf

    awp

    faw

20. oi—oip

    oit

    loi

21. oy—roy

    moy

    foy

22. ou—ouf

23. ow—cow

24. ow—tow

Student's name _____   Date _____

Reversals

Directions: Say, *"Read these words as fast as you can."*

   A student who retains the early tendency of some children to reverse words—*saw* for *was,* *on* for *no,* and so on—will usually slip if reading test words rapidly.

ANSWER SHEET

	Correct	Incorrect
1. pal	_____	_____
2. no	_____	_____
3. saw	_____	_____
4. raw	_____	_____
5. ten	_____	_____
6. tar	_____	_____
7. won	_____	_____
8. pot	_____	_____
9. was	_____	_____
10. on	_____	_____
11. lap	_____	_____
12. tops	_____	_____

Phonics and Structural Analysis

PHONICS TEST
Reversals

1. pal

2. no

3. saw

4. raw

5. ten

6. tar

7. won

8. pot

9. was

10. on

11. lap

12. tops

Structural Analysis

Inflectional Suffixes: Suffixes are usually taught before prefixes and should be added to a word already known by sight. Inflectional suffixes (*s, ed, ing, er, est, ier, y*) are placed at the end of a root for grammatical purposes. They are usually introduced during the latter half of the first grade. This marks the beginning of structural analysis instruction. Children who are able to identify words with inflectional suffixes may then undertake the more complicated task of learning derivational suffixes. If students have difficulty with inflectional suffixes, show them a learned base word and add the suffix to be taught. Present the student with enough examples to clarify the concept.

Objective: ed

play	work	jump
played	worked	jumped

Derivational Suffixes: Derivational suffixes are generally introduced in the second and third grades. Children should be able to see and pronounce the suffix as one unit. Carefully note the specific suffix(es) with which the student has difficulty. Remediation of derivational suffixes is best accomplished through inductive (discovery) teaching. Select the suffix to be taught (e.g., *less*), and add it to several root words the child already knows.

mother	home	tooth
motherless	homeless	toothless

Present the student with additional words containing the suffix to determine if the skill has been transferred.

Prefixes: Prefixes are generally introduced in the second grade after inflectional suffixes and the most common derivational suffixes. Remediate unknown prefixes using the same procedure recommended for derivational suffixes. Select the prefix(es) to be taught, based on the test results. Add the prefix *un* to several known words.

happy	fair	pleasant
unhappy	unfair	unpleasant

Have the student note how the prefix affects the root word. Give additional words for practice.

Student's name _____   Date _____

STRUCTURAL ANALYSIS

Inflectional and Derivational Suffixes and Prefixes

Directions: Nonsense words are used when testing for knowledge of prefixes and suffixes to en-sure that the words are not known by sight. Say, *"Read these nonsense words as well as you can."* Carefully note the specific suffixes and prefixes with which the student experiences difficulty. Mark correct and incorrect responses on the answer sheet (below).

ANSWER SHEET

Inflectional Suffixes	*Prefixes*	
1. s	1. mono	28. mis
2. ed	2. photo	29. co
3. ing	3. poly	30. anti
4. er	4. auto	31. semi
5. est	5. sub	32. trans
6. ly	6. un	
7. ier	7. dis	
	8. in	
Derivational Suffixes	9. pre	
8. ness	10. be	
9. ment	11. non	
10. tion	12. fore	
11. less	13. counter	
12. ful	14. under	
13. ar	15. super	
14. ic	16. tele	
15. ence	17. therm	
16. ship	18. post	
17. age	19. mini	
18. ous	20. photo	
19. ive	21. bi	
20. ant	22. pro	
21. ance	23. en	
22. able	24. ex	
23. hood	25. re	
24. wood	26. con	
	27. de	

Phonics and Structural Analysis

STRUCTURAL ANALYSIS

Inflectional Suffixes

1. flays

2. flayed

3. flaying

4. flayer

5. flayest

6. flayly

7. flaier

Derivational Suffixes

8. bookness

9. carment

10. hilltion

11. drumless

12. bandful

13. lugar

14. felic

15. tendence

16. bendship

17. fileage

18. tubous

19. bandive

20. burnant

21. pondance

22. fourable

23. mildhood

24. bestwood

STRUCTURAL ANALYSIS

Prefixes

1. monotell
2. phototop
3. polygon
4. autogo
5. subman
6. ungo
7. distap
8. inwell
9. prehit
10. besell
11. nongo
12. forehit
13. counterhid
14. undertap
15. supercap
16. telecot

17. thermtop
18. postless
19. minigo
20. photohid
21. biwin
22. prohid
23. enrun
24. exwin
25. recar
26. conmet
27. depan
28. mislead
29. codial
30. antirun
31. semidid
32. transcon

STRUCTURAL ANALYSIS

Compound Words

Directions: Say, "*Read these words as well as you can.*" If the student misses these words, try a trial teaching sequence. Cover the second part of a word and ask for pronunciation of the first part; then cover the first part and ask for pronunciation; finally, uncover the entire word and ask for pronunciation. Ask the student to do the next one independently.

stairway

workhorse

mealtime

carwash

railroad

nightbank

houseboat

headstrong

firehouse

withdrew

outrage

sagebrush

stovepipe

overturned

lollypop

paperjumper

basketmeet

storyteller

screwdriver

dealership

understood

Phonics and Structural Analysis

STRUCTURAL ANALYSIS

Compound Words

stairway

workhorse

mealtime

carwash

railroad

nightbank

houseboat

headstrong

firehouse

withdrew

outrage

sagebrush

stovepipe

overturned

lollypop

paperjumper

basketmeet

storyteller

screwdriver

dealership

understood

PHONICS AND STRUCTURAL ANALYSIS
Testing Record

Phonics

1. *Initial Single Consonants*
   b c d f g h j k l m n p r s t v w z

2. *Consonant Blends*
   bl   br   cl   cr   dr   fr   fl   gl   gr   pl   pr   sc   sk
   sl   sm   sn   sp   st   sw   tr   tw   scr   str

3. *Consonant Digraphs*
   sh   ch   ph   th   wh

4. *Short Vowels*
   a   i   e   o   u

5. *Long Vowels—Silent e Ending*   *Double Vowel Combinations*
   i   o   e   u   a   oa   ea   ai   ee

6. *Vowel Digraphs*
   oo (as in *loose, food*)   oo (as in *cook, stood*)   ew (as in *few, stew*)   au (as in *author*)
   aw (as in *straw*)   oi (as in *oil*)   oy (as in *boy*)   ou (as in *out*)
   ow (as in *cow*)   ow (as in *mow*)

7. *Reversals*
   pal   no   saw   raw   ten   tar
   won   pot   was   on   lap   tops

Structural Analysis

8. *Inflectional Suffixes*
   s   ed   ing   er   est   ly   ier

9. *Derivational Suffixes*
   ness   ment   tion   less   ful   ar   ic   ence   ship
   age   ous   ive   ant   ance   able   hood   wood

10. *Prefixes*
    mono   photo   poly   auto   sub   un   dis   in   pre   be   non
    fore   counter   under   super   tele   therm   post   mini   photo
    bi   pro   en   ex   re   con   de   mis   co   anti   semi   trans

11. *Compound Words*
    stairway   workhorse   mealtime   carwash
    railroad   nightbank   houseboat   headstrong
    firehouse   withdrew   outrage   sagebrush
    stovepipe   overturned   lollypop   paperjumper
    basketmeet   storyteller   screwdriver   dealership   understood

SPELLING TESTS

Seven word lists are provided in the Diagnostic Spelling tests (pp. 107–109) so that the examiner can obtain diagnostic information related to the student's ability to spell. Only 10 words are included in each test, to prevent fatigue or discouragement. Therefore, additional evidence of student performance must be gathered from his or her writing to confirm hypotheses about the student in regard to cognitive development in encoding language; sound-symbol association; auditory discrimination, memory, and sequencing; visual discrimination, memory, and sequencing; and knowledge of common rules and conventions. The spelling tests can serve as a quick phonics assessment.

Administration

Select only the test or tests that appear to be appropriate to the area being explored and the reading level of the student. For example, give tests one and three to nonreaders and those below the third-grade reading level. Move to easier or more difficult lists as necessary. For each test, give the student a separate sheet of lined paper, numbered from one to ten. Say, *"I want you to write some words for me, please. If there are some words you don't know, just try to spell them as well as you can. I will say each word, use it in a sentence, and say it again. Then you are to write the word. Remember to wait until I say the word the last time before you start to write."* The examiner may repeat the word and encourage the student to *"try it even if you aren't sure,"* and *"you can say it as you write it,"* but no other prompting, such as sounding by word parts, is permitted. This test may be administered to groups.

Interpretation

Lists One and Two, Phonetic Spelling

Lists one and two can be used to determine whether students can discriminate sounds, associate sounds with letters, and write sounds in sequence. Students may have memorized some words in these and other lists; consider this in interpretation. In addition to analyzing the student's production, note whether the student said the words or sounds of the letters before, during, or after writing as an aid to production.

Lists Three and Four, Nonphonetic Spelling

Lists three and four can be used to determine whether students can make fine visual discriminations within words, recall visual letter forms, and reproduce them in sequence. Note attempts to visually recall the word before writing to see if it "looks right." These lists may also be used to learn whether the student attempts to recall the word by reciting the names rather than the sounds of the letters before, during, or after writing the words.

Lists Five and Six, Spelling Rules and Conventions

Lists five and six sample students' knowledge of spelling rules and conventions. These can be learned inductively by students who discover patterns in derived words they read and write. Some students may have had some instruction in rules and can be heard reciting, "*i* before *e* . . . " or "change the *y* to *i*. . . . " Words missed on parts reflecting a common spelling pattern should be rechecked by testing with similar words. Those patterns not known may be acquired through practice with similar derived forms. Rules may be useful to those with poor visual discrimination and memory. (Some words on this test may have been memorized by the students and do not reflect their mastery of a spelling rule or convention.)

List Seven, High-Frequency Words Commonly Misspelled

List seven contains words that older students with spelling difficulties often misspell. Because these are high-frequency function words, their use cannot be avoided. Older students may have written these words incorrectly so often that the misspelling no longer appears to be incorrect or different from the correct spelling they see in printed materials. In addition to the 10 words on this list, the examiner should check the student's writing for frequently misspelled words.

SUMMARIZING STUDENT SPELLING PERFORMANCE

The foregoing lists and samples of the student's writing can be used to make a detailed analysis of spelling performance. A checklist for this purpose appears on page 110.

COGNITIVE DEVELOPMENT AS A BASIS FOR SELECTING A REMEDIAL READING APPROACH

In their self-evaluations, practicing teachers and reading specialists, as well as those completing their master's degree in reading, frequently mention the need for more guidelines in selecting an appropriate instructional approach for readers who are severely disabled. One hesitates to give a simplistic set of rules because of the number of factors that can influence the efficacy of a particular approach (e.g., emotional problems, impaired vision or hearing, language problems, previous instruction, neurological difficulties). Nevertheless, there are some indicators of cognitive development with regard to writing words that seem to be helpful to teachers who are planning remediation.

The following case excerpts illustrate a fairly typical kind of analysis that has been useful in deciding whether to try a Fernald Language Experience Approach (LEA) or an alternative approach with certain students with reading difficulties. Table 1 contains the attempts of four children to write the list of words that were dictated to them.

TABLE 1
Words Written from Dictation: Four Children

Words Dictated	JON 8 Yr., 0 Mo. RL: PP ML: 3.0	TIM 7 Yr., 8 Mo. RL: PP ML: 2.5	JEFF 8 Yr., 9 Mo. RL: PP ML: 2.0	TRISHA 7 Yr., 6 Mo. RL: PP ML: 2.0
1. go	go	po	G	go
2. pad	pD	pd	p	pad
3. set	ct	sct	S	set
4. fed	yD*	ft	f	fed
5. pep	PP	pt	p	pep
6. last	LccD	Lt	L	last
7. find	yD*	fv	f	fid
8. chip	Cep	Pi	—	chip
9. wish	—	A	—	wish
10. bus	Bcc	BS	b	bus

*Consistently wrote *y* for *A*.

RL = Reading Level

ML = Math Level

Table 2 contains a guide to the development of the ability to write words. Although there is much variability from child to child, generally the sequence that can be observed is one that moves from a representation of the first sound in a word, to the addition of the final consonant sound, and finally to the representation of vowels. This progression in children's learning has been described by Henderson and Beers (1980). The author has found that adult beginning readers tend to follow the same sequence. Five stages of spelling development are identified by Bear, Invernizzi, Templeton, and Johnston (2004). The stages are emergent spelling, letter-name spelling, within-word pattern spelling, syllables and affixes spelling, and derivational relationships.

TABLE 2
Cognitive Development in Writing Words

Approximate Grade Level	Pencil	Bed	Make
K–1.0	P	B	M
1.5	PSL	BD	MK
1.9	PWSL	BAD	MAEK
2.0	PNSAL	BED	MAKE

Jon, Tim, and Jeff have learned to perform simple tasks in addition and subtraction, indicating that they have the ability to learn. They can recognize very few words, but they can discriminate and represent the beginning sound in a word. Jeff, however, has not reached the level of Jon and Tim in word knowledge, as they can write the final sound in some words and Jeff cannot. The three boys have had psychological evaluations that report full-scale IQs from 81 to 90. They are in regular classrooms.

Jon, Tim, and Jeff were guided through the standard VAKT-Language Experience Approach described by Fernald (1943). With only a few trials, Jon and Tim were writing words and reading them in their experience stories. Jeff required many trials and needed much support in reading the stories he dictated. It seemed apparent that Jeff's knowledge of words had not developed to the stage where the Fernald approach would be the most effective. Therefore, Jeff was given some structured guidance in the study of one-syllable words. The Hegge, Kirk, and Kirk (1965) word patterns were used, although any similar material would have sufficed. Although initially Jeff needed to keep a picture before him to remind him of the medial vowel sound, he was soon competently sorting words, creating rhymes, and fluently reading the beginning drills. This guided word study helped Jeff move to the level of phonological competence that he needed to be successful in beginning reading instruction.

Trisha was 7 years, 6 months in the eighth month of first grade. She had been evaluated by the school psychologist, who reported her scores as indicating borderline mental impairment. An occupational therapist described Trisha as functioning slightly below level in development of spatial organization and balance. A speech therapist had been helping Trisha overcome articulation problems. Trisha's major difficulty in the classroom was following directions. The same behavior was noted during testing. She needed repeated explanations, supported with visual aids.

Trisha's reading level in context, oral and silent, and on the word list test was preprimer. She did not use context in reading; given the oral cloze test for beginning readers, Trisha correctly completed only three of eight. A sample of Trisha's speech was taped and transcribed. She was able to use short sentences correctly, but her language became grammatically incorrect and difficult to understand when she attempted longer sentences. Trisha did well on sentence repetition and syntax matching tests.

On the dictated spelling list, Trisha missed only one word. She omitted the *n* in *find.* The results of the phonics inventory indicated good sound-symbol knowledge. Trisha could discriminate and associate consonants and consonant blends as well as short and long vowels.

Since the major impediment to growth reading seemed to be Trisha's language processing difficulties, a holistic reading approach was selected that employed neurological impress procedures for the first stage of remediation. After four weeks, Trisha's reading was greatly improved and she was able to move from preprimer to first-grade material. Later, Trisha's fluency and confidence were aided with prepared oral reading and participation in choral reading activities. When Trisha started to use LEA, she was given instruction in sentence expansions.

While one hesitates to say that the selection of remedial approach is limited only to the factors presented here, Jon, Tim, and Jeff are representative of a number of children one sees in the clinical setting. Teachers seem to find the analysis of writing to be helpful in selecting a starting point for instruction for these children.

Children such as Trisha present a difficult challenge. Teachers are puzzled when they see an adequate development of phonological understanding but a lack of development in more holistic processing. Generally, the situation is reversed. For these children, analysis of receptive language, oral language, and written language is required in order to make a decision about remedial approaches.

References

References are included for the classic, original descriptions of methodology. Generally, more recent writers condense their presentations of these methods resulting in the methods not always being used effectively. Readers are encouraged to read original documents, as well as more current interpretations and adaptations.

Bader, L. A. (1980). *Reading diagnosis and remediation in classroom and clinic.* New York: Macmillan.

Bear, D. R., Invernizzi, M., Templeton, S., & Johnston, F. (2004). *Words their way: Word study for phonics, vocabulary, and spelling instruction,* (3rd ed.). Upper Saddle River, NJ: Merrill/Prentice Hall.

Fernald, G. M. (1943). *Remedial techniques in basic school subjects.* New York: McGraw-Hill.

Gunning, T. G. (2002). *Assessing and correcting reading and writing difficulties,* (2nd ed.). Boston: Allyn & Bacon.

Heckleman, R. G. (1969). Using the neurological impress remedial reading technique. *Academic Therapy Quarterly,* I, (4).

Hegge, T. G., Kirk, S. A., & Kirk, W. D. (1965). *Remedial marking drills.* Ann Arbor, MI: George Wahr.

Henderson, E., & Beers, J. (Eds.). (1980). *Developmental and cognitive aspects of learning to spell: A reflection of word knowledge.* Newark, DE: International Reading Association.

McCormick, S. (2003). *Instructing students who have literacy problems,* (4th ed.). Upper Saddle River, NJ: Merrill/Prentice Hall.

Methods useful to tutors and beginning teachers may be found in:

Bader, L. A. (1998). *Read to succeed literacy tutor's manual.* Upper Saddle River, NJ: Merrill/Prentice Hall.

Spelling Tests

DIAGNOSTIC SPELLING TESTS

Directions: Pronounce the word, use the word in a sentence, and repeat the word.

LIST ONE:
Words Spelled Phonetically, Requiring Ability to Hear and Write Sounds

Reading Levels P–2.0

1.	go	Where did he go?
2.	pad	I have a pad of paper.
3.	sit	Please sit here.
4.	fed	I fed my dog.
5.	pep	A cheerleader has pep.
6.	last	This is my last piece of paper.
7.	find	I can't find it.
8.	chip	There is a chip out of this cup.
9.	wish	Make a wish.
10.	bus	We rode the bus.

LIST TWO:
Words Spelled Phonetically, Requiring Ability to Hear and Write Sounds

Reading Levels 3+

1.	flash	Here is a flashlight.
2.	thump	I heard a thump.
3.	wind	The wind blows.
4.	strap	The strap broke.
5.	twist	Twist the strings together to make a rope.
6.	rent	The house is for rent.
7.	boots	She put on her boots.
8.	child	The child is four years old.
9.	split	The man split wood for a fire.
10.	mouth	You must take care of the teeth in your mouth.

LIST THREE:
Words with Silent Letters, Requiring Visual Memory

Reading Levels P–2.0

1.	one	I have one pencil.
2.	eat	Eat an apple.
3.	were	We were outside.
4.	ice	They have some ice cream.
5.	may	May I help you?
6.	here	He is not here.
7.	happy	They are happy.
8.	little	I saw a little dog.
9.	come	Come to my house.
10.	they	They are not here.

LIST FOUR:
Words with Silent Letters, Requiring Visual Memory

Reading Levels 3+

1. store	We went to the store.
2. listen	Listen to the music.
3. high	How high can you jump?
4. laugh	She made me laugh.
5. write	Will you write me a letter?
6. hour	We were there an hour.
7. know	Do you know how to skate?
8. loaf	I bought a loaf of bread.
9. would	Would you go with me?
10. light	Please turn on the light.

LIST FIVE:
Words Illustrating Common Spelling Rules and Conventions
(may also reflect visual memory)

Reading Levels 2–4

1. stopped	She stopped the car.
2. glasses	Do you wear glasses?
3. coming	He is coming home.
4. flies	My friend flies a plane.
5. cookie	I ate a cookie.
6. cutting	We will be cutting wood.
7. hoped	I hoped you would come.
8. using	Are you using your ruler?
9. finally	We finally went home.
10. beginning	We were beginning to get tired.

LIST SIX:
Words Illustrating Common Spelling Rules or Conventions

Reading Levels 5+

1. equally	The pie was divided equally.
2. musician	The violinist is a fine musician.
3. knives	We need more forks and knives.
4. usefulness	The usefulness of this tool has been established.
5. humorous	The stores were humorous.
6. impression	He tried to make a good impression.
7. receive	Did you receive a letter?
8. factories	The factories are on the edge of town.
9. substantial	She made a substantial investment.
10. immeasurable	The amount was immeasurable.

Spelling Tests

LIST SEVEN:
High-Frequency Words Commonly Misspelled

Reading Levels 4+

1. been	Where have you been?
2. when	When will you be ready?
3. does	How does that work?
4. were	Were you at the game?
5. because	He smiled because he was happy.
6. what	What colors do you like?
7. know	So you know that person?
8. many	Many people went to the game.
9. their	This is their home.
10. too	We ate too much.

SUMMARY OF SPELLING PERFORMANCE

Student's name _____ Date _____

Yes/No

_____ Ability to hear and represent sounds developed on level with peers.

Developmental Stage: _____

_____ Prephonetic: _____ Scribble: _____ Random letters: _____ Emergent: _____

_____ Letter-name strategy: _____ Initial letter: _____ Initial and final consonant: _____

_____ Letter combinations: _____ Transitional to correct forms: _____

Knowledge of Phonetic Elements

_____ Consonants. Unknown: _____

_____ Vowels. Unknown (long and short): _____

_____ Consonant combinations. Unknown: _____

_____ Vowel combinations. Unknown: _____

Spelling Behaviors   *Examples*

_____ Omits sounded letters _____

_____ Omits silent letters _____

_____ Adds letters, phonetically acceptable _____

_____ Adds letters, not phonetically acceptable _____

_____ Transposes order of silent letters _____

_____ Transposes order of sounded letters _____

_____ Phonetic substitutions, consonants _____

_____ Phonetic substitutions, vowels _____

_____ Nonphonetic substitutions, consonants _____

_____ Nonphonetic substitutions, vowels _____

_____ Substitutions reflect accurate representation of dialect _____

_____

_____ Lacks knowledge of common rules or conventions _____

_____

_____ Needs help with high-frequency words used in writing _____

_____

Examiner's conclusions: _____

_____

_____

(See the Preliteracy Assessment Testing Record on p. 130.)

Spelling Tests

VISUAL AND AUDITORY DISCRIMINATION

The Visual Discrimination tests and the Auditory Discrimination of Word Pairs test are aids to identify learners with difficulties in vision and hearing. In many educational settings resources for assessing vision and hearing are limited, but efforts should be made to obtain help for learners whose progress is impeded by poor vision or hearing.

The results of these tests should not be the only determinant of the learner's abilities in vision and hearing. The tests should be used in conjunction with observations, interviews, and with telebinocular and audiometric screening. Referrals should be made to appropriate professionals for more thorough evaluation when there appears to be a problem.

VISUAL DISCRIMINATION TESTS

Two tests of visual discrimination are provided. They both require the student to match letters and words. The first test, Visual Discrimination I, may be used with nonreaders and beginning readers on levels PP–1. Visual Discrimination II may be used with students reading on level 2 and above. Rubin (2002) recommends visual discrimination tasks using letters rather than geometric forms.

Directions: Say, *"On this paper you are to look at the letter, word, or phrase after the number, and circle the following items that are the same. In some parts there will be more than one item that is the same; circle them all. First do the practice line (example)."* Give help as needed. When the student understands the task, say, *"Begin."* Time the student, unobtrusively. Permit her or him to take as much time as necessary to complete the task.

Interpretation: Note whether time to complete the task and number of errors are excessive in comparison with peers. Problems may be indicated by head close to page, matching letter by letter, using fingers to hold place, constant rechecking, erasing. A general guide: PP and level 1 readers should take no more than 3 minutes to complete Visual Discrimination I; level 2 and above readers should take no more than 3 minutes to complete Visual Discrimination II. The difficulty that nonreaders often have with tasks 7 and 8 may not be related to visual difficulties.

An activity in the author's experience that has identified discreprencies in near point and far point visual abilities is to ask the student to copy a passage from far point and copy another passage of equal length from near point. Note the time required as well as the student's behaviors.

VISUAL DISCRIMINATION I

Example: O   K   W   O   X

1. V   N   A   W   V

2. a   g   e   a   o   u   a

3. d   d p b g d p b

4. on   ua no om mo on

5. saw   mas saw was sam saw

6. flag   flay flog flag lafg flay

7. at me   to me   te mo   at we   at me
                          ot me   at me   it me   at ne

8. stop the car   stop tha car   stop the cow   stop the car
                          stop the car   pots the car   stod the car
                          stop the rac   stob the car   stop the car

VISUAL DISCRIMINATION II

Example: B   A   C   B   O   P   X   B   L   M   N   O   B   C

1. a   g   f   j   c   e   a   l   m   n   e
            o   l   b   q   a   b   a   c   x

2. ralg   ralg   role   rall   raly   rolg   raly
            ralg   rolg   raly   rapg   rabg

3. flag   flay   fbly   flag   plag   flug   fbov
            blag   plag   flag   flug   flog

4. Eastern   Andron High   Eastern High   Eostern High   Eastern Heyl
   High   Eistern High   Eastern Hiyl   Eastern High   Eustern High

5. round   ring the bend   round the bowl   round the bend
   the bend round the bind   round thi bend   round tha bend
            rouse the bend   round the bend   round the bend
            around the bend   round the bind   round the pend

6. BEST   BENT   BEST   BENT   BECT   BEST   BEIT
            BEST   BESF   BIST   BEST   BINH

7. everybody everybody   everydoby   ewerybody   everybaby
              everybody   evevybody   everybody   evarybody

AUDITORY DISCRIMINATION TEST

The Auditory Discrimination of Word Pairs test requires the student to listen to two words to determine if they are alike or different. The examiner can obtain information to help determine whether the student should be referred for a hearing test and whether the student might have difficulty in hearing fine sound differences so that letter-sound association instruction would be impeded.

Directions: Place the student so he or she cannot see the examiner's face. Say, *"I am going to say some words for you. Listen so you can tell me if the words are the same or different."* If the examiner has reason to doubt the student's understanding of same or different, say, *"**Same** means I said it two times. **Big, big.** I said **big** two times. They were the same words. Now listen. **Big, twig.** I said two **different** words. Tell me what same words and different words mean."* When the student understands same and different, begin the test.

Before giving the test, practice saying the word pairs so that inflection and emphasis are the same on each pair of words. It may be helpful to practice with a tape recorder to ensure a clear enunciation that does not provide clues to the listener.

Scoring and Interpretation: Total the number of errors. Six-year-old children should make no more than six errors; seven-year-old children, no more than five errors; and those eight years old or older, no more than four errors. This assumes an attentive, cooperative student without a cold, allergy, or other temporary physical problems; optimum, quiet testing conditions; and careful test administration. The examiner may wish to examine the words on which the errors occurred. The letters in front of each word pair indicate the location of the difference: *B*—beginning; *M*—middle; *E*—ending. An *S* is used if the pair is the same. Students with some kinds of high-frequency hearing loss may have difficulty with consonants, especially ending sounds; those with low-frequency loss may have difficulty hearing the middle sounds (vowels). Research indicates that auditory discrimination of speech sounds continues to develop until about age eight. Results of this test may indicate the need for further testing of auditory discrimination or testing of auditory acuity.

Student's name _____   Date _____

AUDITORY DISCRIMINATION OF WORD PAIRS

1. (M)   big—bag   ____   16. (M)   lip—lap   ____

2. (E)   lease—leash   ____   17. (E)   dim—din   ____

3. (S)   pot—pot   ____   18. (S)   king—king   ____

4. (B)   latch—patch   ____   19. (B)   dump—lump   ____

5. (S)   bus—bus   ____   20. (S)   live—live   ____

6. (M)   fest—fast   ____   21. (E)   much—mush   ____

7. (E)   muff—muss   ____   22. (M)   ton—ten   ____

8. (S)   tiger—tiger   ____   23. (B)   chair—pair   ____

9. (M)   rope—rap   ____   24. (E)   mouth—mouse   ____

10. (B)   glad—dad   ____   25. (M)   pet—pat   ____

11. (M)   noon—none   ____   26. (E)   sheaf—sheath   ____

12. (E)   cat—cap   ____   27. (S)   fed—fed   ____

13. (B)   fun—run   ____   28. (B)   tug—lug   ____

14. (S)   man—man   ____   29. (M)   led—lad   ____

15. (B)   shack—lack   ____   30. (B)   past—last   ____

Word pair differences:

8 middle

7 ending

8 beginning

Word pairs the same: 7

PRELITERACY AND EMERGING LITERACY ASSESSMENT

This section is designed to ascertain strengths and needs of students who are unable to read the graded word lists or passages. The tests are provided to give the examiner specific information regarding preliteracy and emerging literacy skills. Included are tests to assess the metalinguistic skills of literacy awareness. Letter and phonemic knowledge and manipulation tests are on pages 71–84. Literacy awareness deals with the student's ability to understand concepts related to reading, while manipulation refers to abilities such as isolating and blending segments of language.

Oral language and early print awareness are assessed with syntax word matching tests and semantic and syntactic cloze tests. Spelling test one (p. 107) may be given to assess phonemic applications through invented spelling. Visual discrimination and auditory discrimination tests are presented to rule out disabilities in these areas.

A testing record is provided on page 130.

LITERACY AWARENESS:
ASSESSMENT OF BEGINNING CONCEPTS ABOUT PRINT

Directions: The following Literacy Concepts interviews require a child's book, paper, and markers or pencil.

Interpretation: Record acquired and unacquired concepts for use in remediation. These concepts are best developed over time, by incorporating explanations into literacy lessons.

Student's name _____   Date _____

LITERACY CONCEPTS—INTERVIEW I

Directions: In the blank space provided, write *A* for acceptable or *NA* for not acceptable.

1. Hand the child the book so that it is upside down and backward from his or her point of view. Say, "*Let's look at this book.*" Observe whether the child turns the book upright. If the child does not spontaneously turn the book over and open it at the beginning, say, "*Where does this book start?*"

    Child turns book upright _____

    Child correctly identifies beginning of book _____

2. Ask the child to tell you what is happening in the book. If the child is unable or unwilling to do so, offer to read the book.

    Child produces a plausible narrative _____

3. After the child has narrated a few pages (or the examiner has read a few pages), pause and ask the child, "*Where does it say that?*"

    Child points to printed text _____

4. If the child successfully points to printed text, ask him or her to point to a word.

    Child points to a single word _____

5. Give the child a clean sheet of paper and a selection of colored markers and pencils. Ask him or her to *draw something*. When the child has completed the drawing, or after a few minutes, remove the first paper, give the child another clean sheet of paper, and ask him or her to write something. Record the child's comments during each activity. Note whether the child's intent appears to be appropriate to each task (e.g., when writing). Look for evidence of distinction between drawing and writing in the finished products (e.g., linear forms for writing versus circular forms for drawing, or vice versa).

    Child distinguishes between drawing and writing _____

Student's name _____   Date _____

LITERACY CONCEPTS—INTERVIEW II

Directions: Write *A* for acceptable or *NA* for not acceptable on the blank.

A/NA	Concept	Directions
_____	page	Say, *"Please turn the page"* or *"Name the picture on any page."*
_____	letter	Say, *"Can you point to any letter on this page?"* or write down three symbols (& % B) and say: *"Pick the one that's a letter."*
_____	word	Write three words in a row and say, *"Circle any word."* (e.g., *How are you?*)
_____	line	Say, *"Point to any line on the page, run your finger until the line is finished."*
_____	first/last/middle	Say, *"Point to the first and last word on the page."* Show three words and say, *"Point to the first word." "Point to the second word." "Point to the last word."*
_____	before/after	Indicate any word on the page. Say, *"I have my finger on this word. You point to the word before this word." "Point to the word after this word."* (If not known, use three physical objects.)
_____	top/bottom	Say, *"Look at this page. Point to the top of the page. Point to the bottom of the page."* (If not known, use a glass.)
_____	above	Point to a line in the middle of the page. Say, *"Look at the line where my finger is. Point to the line above. Point to the line below."* (If not known, use a physical object.)
_____	sentence	Read a short paragraph to the child. Before beginning, say, *"I am going to read to you some sentences. When I have finished the first one, hold up your hand."*

Student's name _____   Date _____

SYNTAX (WORD) MATCHING

This task may be used with nonreaders. It tests the ability of the student to recognize words as separate speech entities within sentences.

Syntax Matching Test

This says:	You say it.	Say it again.	Point to:
Close the door.	"	"	close
Pet the dog.	"	"	dog
See his new hat.	"	"	new
Her puppy is barking.	"	"	barking
This horse can run fast.	"	"	run
You can go with me.	"	"	with

Number correct _____

Interpretation: A score of at least four correct words can serve as one indication that the child is aware of separate words in sentences and that these can be printed sequentially. Discount the score if the child appears to be guessing. Since this is a brief sample of one ability, other indications of reading readiness, such as naming and writing letters, should be considered.

SYNTAX MATCHING TEST

Example A	**Go home.**
Example B	**Look out.**
1.	**Close the door.**
2.	**Pet the dog.**
3.	**See his new hat.**
4.	**Her puppy is barking.**
5.	**This horse can run fast.**
6.	**You can go with me.**

SEMANTIC AND SYNTACTIC EVALUATION: CLOZE TESTS

Cloze tests may be given to determine if students are able to use semantic and syntactic cues as aids to comprehension and word identification. Students use semantic cues if their previous experiences and meaning vocabulary enable them to predict an upcoming word in a sentence. For example, in the sentence

When the tire blew, the car immediately veered toward the side of the road.

a reader may substitute for *car* any of the following words: *auto, motor car, vehicle, sedan, jalopy, lemon* and still retain the general meaning. This type of substitution indicates that the reader uses semantic cues.

Syntactic cues are based on the syntax of the sentence. In order to use these, a reader must have a developed language structure. If in the example the reader read *dog* for *car*, the reader would be using syntactic cues because he or she substituted one noun for another. While readers generally use both cue systems concurrently, it is helpful to determine the extent to which each is emphasized.

Included in the next section are four cloze subtests. Cloze I (Cloze Test for Beginning Readers) is intended for those students reading from primer through second-grade levels and examines their abilities to use context as an aid to word identification and comprehension. Cloze II (Semantic Cloze) may be given to children ranging from nonreaders to those reading on a primary level and is designed to measure the child's level of cultural experiences as well as language development, association, retrieval, and expression. Cloze III (Syntactic Cloze Test) is recommended for students reading at or above the second-grade level and measures the reader's sentence structure development and ability to use syntax in making predictions. Cloze IV (Grammatical Closure) is designed to assess mastery of grammatical forms for students who are language delayed or ELL.

CLOZE TEST FOR BEGINNING READERS (CLOZE I)

Purpose and Level: This supplementary test may be given to students reading on primer through second-grade levels to examine their abilities to use context as an aid to comprehension.

Administration: If capable, the student should read the sentence. However, if he or she is unable to do so, the examiner may read while the child listens. Have the child point to the words as they are read.

Directions: Say, *"This story has some words missing. Try to read the story by guessing the missing words."* If the child is unable to read the passage, say, *"I will read each line of the story. You point to each word I say. Try to guess the missing word."* Repeat lines as necessary.

Scoring and Interpretation: Any word that is semantically and syntactically suitable is acceptable; however, it must be suitable in the context of the entire paragraph. For example, if sentence 6 (But they do not _____ too much.) is taken out of context, such words as *eat, drive,* or *play* would be acceptable. Within the context of the entire paragraph, however, they would be incorrect semantically. The following are some possible correct answers. The examiner may determine that other substitutions are both semantically and syntactically correct as well.

1.   The rain came down all _____. (*day, night, evening*)

2.   We could not go _____. (*out, outside*)

3.   We wanted the rain to _____. (*stop, slow down*)

4.   _____ makes plants grow. (*Rain, Water*)

5.   Farmers _____ the rain. (*want, need*)

6.   But they do not _____ too much. (*need, want, desire*)

7.   Too much _____ can kill the _____. (*rain, water; crops, potatoes*)

Student's name _____   Date _____

ANSWER SHEET—RESPONSES

	Semantically		*Syntactically*	
acceptable	*not acceptable*	*acceptable*	*not acceptable*	
1. _____	_____	_____	_____	
2. _____	_____	_____	_____	
3. _____	_____	_____	_____	
4. _____	_____	_____	_____	
5. _____	_____	_____	_____	
6. _____	_____	_____	_____	
7. _____	_____	_____	_____	
8. _____	_____	_____	_____	

Students should be able to guess at least five words out of eight. Students who have unusual difficulty in pointing to words as the sentences are read aloud may not have developed an appropriate concept of a word.

Semantic and Syntactic Evaluation

1. The rain came down all _____ .

2. We could not go _____ .

3. We wanted the rain to _____ .

4. _____ makes plants grow.

5. Farmers _____ the rain.

6. But they do not _____ too much.

7. Too much _____ can kill the

8. _____ .

SEMANTIC CLOZE TEST (CLOZE II)

Purpose and Level: This test may be given to nonreaders or those on a primary level. It contains 10 sentences that students should be able to complete based on their background of experiences. Those who have difficulty may not have had the cultural experiences implicit in the sentences, or they may have problems in language development, association, retrieval, or expression.

Administration: The examiner reads the sentences to the student. If he or she is unable to respond, supply the correct answer and then proceed with the next sentence. Stop if the student misses three.

Directions: Say, *"I will read some sentences with the last word missing. Try to guess the missing word. Let's do one for practice. 'He jumped up and _____.'"* If the student does not respond appropriately, say, *"Down. He jumped up and down. Let's try this one."*

Scoring and Interpretation: Accept reasonable guesses. Children between 6 and 8 should miss no more than five. Older students should miss no more than three.

Discuss missed items that may reflect a lack of experience. If experiential background is ruled out as a source of inability to respond, further evaluation of language facility may be indicated.

Since shyness, hostility, or refusal to cooperate may be a factor, other observations should be made before referring the student.

The following are some possible correct answers. The examiner may determine that other substitutions are semantically and syntactically correct as well.

Student's name _____   Date _____

1. door, window, drawer
2. brother
3. hot
4. hospital
5. change
6. mat, rug
7. drawer
8. cool, cold
9. cry, scream
10. race, game, contest

Semantic and Syntactic Evaluation

SEMANTIC CLOZE TEST (CLOZE II)

1. Please close the _____ .

2. She has one sister and one _____ .

3. I burned my tongue because the soup was _____ .

4. He hurt his leg and went to the emergency room at the _____ .

5. I waited at the crosswalk for the light to _____ .

6. Please wipe your feet on the _____ .

7. Put your clothes in the dresser _____ .

8. She put on a coat because she was _____ .

9. A loud noise made the baby _____ .

10. The team was happy because they won the _____ .

SYNTACTIC CLOZE TEST (CLOZE III)

Purpose and Level: This test is more difficult than Cloze II and is recommended for students reading at or above the second-grade level. The purpose is to determine which sentence parts the student finds difficult. This test contains 10 sentences that require the student to guess a missing word that is both semantically and syntactically correct.

Administration: The student reads each sentence, first silently, then orally, supplying the missing word.

Directions: Say, "*These sentences have some words missing. Try to guess what they are. Read each sentence to yourself, then read it to me.*"

Scoring and Interpretation: Accept reasonable guesses that fit the meaning and the part of speech required. Make a record of sentence parts that are difficult for the student.

Student's name _____   Date _____

1.   He waited for his _____. (*noun*)

2.   Your new shirt is _____. (*adjective*)

3.   I can't _____ very fast. (*verb*)

4.   She gave _____ mother some flowers. (*pronoun*)

5.   I like hot dogs, _____ I like hamburgers better. (*conjunction*)

6.   Talk _____ so they can't hear you. (*adverb*)

7.   Put the cup _____ the table. (*preposition*)

8.   They like baseball _____ football. (*conjunction*)

9.   The dog _____ barking. (*verb*)

10.   He came here _____ another city. (*preposition*)

Semantic and Syntactic Evaluation

SYNTACTIC CLOZE TEST (CLOZE III)

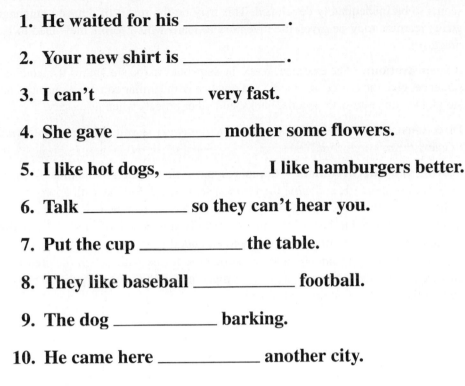

1. He waited for his _____ .

2. Your new shirt is _____ .

3. I can't _____ very fast.

4. She gave _____ mother some flowers.

5. I like hot dogs, _____ I like hamburgers better.

6. Talk _____ so they can't hear you.

7. Put the cup _____ the table.

8. They like baseball _____ football.

9. The dog _____ barking.

10. He came here _____ another city.

GRAMMATICAL CLOSURE (CLOZE IV)

Purpose and Level: The grammatical closure test may be given to students whose speech seems to be inadequately developed. This may be the result of delayed language. English language learners may be given the inventory to learn which forms may need to be reviewed and practiced.

Administration: The examiner reads the sentences to the student. If the student misses the first sentence, give the correct response, and practice with similar constructions until the task is understood. Demonstrate with pencils, books, and other objects when necessary.

Directions: Say, "*I am going to read some sentences to you that have some words missing. Try to guess the missing word.*"

Scoring and Interpretation: Accept responses that fit the grammatical form, such as *pens* for *pencils* in sentence 1, and *mine* for *yours* in sentence 2. Repeat with appropriate demonstration if the student gives a response such as *shoes* for *feet* in sentence 10. Make a record of grammatical forms that need to be taught. Since this test is quite short, other samples of the student's language may need to be obtained. The recommended procedure is to tape a sample of about 200 words, transcribe the sample, and categorize the forms with which the student is having difficulty. Compare the student's language competency with his or her peers. Refer to a speech therapist if the problems seem to be severe.

GRAMMATICAL CLOSURE (CLOZE IV)

1. This is a pencil. Here are two _____. (*plural*)

2. This is my pencil. That pencil is _____. (*possessive pronoun*)

3. I can tap my pencil. Now I am _____. (*present participle*)

4. I saw one man. Then I saw three _____. (*plural*)

5. The child breaks his toys. Now all of the toys have been _____. (*past participle*)

6. This book belongs to Nancy. Whose book is it? It is _____. (*possessive*)

7. I have a box and you have a box. We have two _____. (*plural*)

8. This book is on the table. Where is this book? (*demonstrate over or under*)

   _____ the table. (*preposition*)

9. This book is big. This one is bigger. And this one is the _____. (*comparative*

   adjective)

10. This is a foot. Here are two _____. (*plural*)

11. He said he would go; now he has _____. (*past participle*)

12. She was writing. Look at what she has _____. (*past participle*)

13. Mary has many pencils, but Sue has even _____. (*comparative adjective*)

14. I saw a mouse; then I saw two _____. (*plural*)

15. Tim enjoyed himself at the party. Tina enjoyed herself. They both enjoyed

    _____. (*plural possessive*)

Student's name _____ Date _____

PRELITERACY/EMERGENT LITERACY ASSESSMENT RECORD

Testing Record	Unsatisfactory	Satisfactory	Specific Needs
1. Literacy Concepts	_____	_____	_____
2. Rhyme Recognition	_____	_____	_____
3. Initial Phoneme Recognition	_____	_____	_____
4. Blending Phonemes	_____	_____	_____
5. Segmenting Phonemes	_____	_____	_____
6. Letter Knowledge:			
a. Recognition	_____	_____	_____
b. Identification	_____	_____	_____
c. Reproduction	_____	_____	_____
7. Hearing Letter Names in Words	_____	_____	_____
8. Syntax (Word) Matching	_____	_____	_____
9. Cloze Tests:			
Cloze Test I	_____	_____	_____
Cloze Test II	_____	_____	_____
Cloze Test III	_____	_____	_____
Cloze Test IV	_____	_____	_____
10. Visual Discrimination	_____	_____	_____
11. Auditory Discrimination	_____	_____	_____
12. Spelling, Test 1:			
a. Beginning Consonant	_____	_____	_____
b. Ending Consonant	_____	_____	_____
c. Medial Vowel	_____	_____	_____

Semantic and Syntactic Evaluation

ORAL LANGUAGE ASSESSMENT

Evaluation of Expression

Several methods may be employed to elicit oral language. The strategy or strategies used will depend on which aspects of language need to be evaluated and the degree of development. The following procedures are recommended.

Describing: Show the student a picture suitable to her or his maturity, with three or more actors (people or animals) engaged in easily recognized activities. Say, *"Please look at the picture and tell me as much as you can about it."* As necessary, encourage the student to continue. Say, *"Good, tell me some more"* or *"Fine, go on."* If at all possible, tape the student; then transcribe the tape. If a tape cannot be made, write the student's utterances. A show-and-tell activity might be used if the student is not intimidated by being in front of a group. Analyze the speech sample and record the results on the Oral Language Expression Checklist (p. 132).

Retelling: Read to the student a passage of 60 to 100 words, suitable in length and content to the student's maturity and interest. The passage should have a well-organized content. Ask the student to retell the story. Tape, transcribe, and analyze the performance as outlined in procedure 1 and record results on the checklist. (Retelling information may also be obtained from highest independent-level performance on graded passages.)

Dictating: Have the student make up a story and dictate it to the examiner. Pictures or opening sentences (story starters) may be used to stimulate the student. Analyze and record the results on the Oral Language Expression Checklist (on p. 132).

Student's name _____ Date _____

ORAL LANGUAGE EXPRESSION CHECKLIST

Yes	No	Comparison with Peers Indicates Satisfactory Performance in:	Description and Examples of Problems
_____	_____	Articulation	
_____	_____	English as a second language	
_____	_____	Fluency	
_____	_____	Volume	
_____	_____	Voice quality	
_____	_____	Other speech areas	

Vocabulary Development

_____	_____	Understanding of connotation	
_____	_____	Definition by use (*chair*—sit on it)	
_____	_____	Definition by description (has four legs)	
_____	_____	Definition by category (furniture)	

Level of Abstraction

_____	_____	Description of action or quality	
_____	_____	Interpretation of actions or events	
_____	_____	Prediction of actions or events	
_____	_____	Evaluation of actions or events	

Syntactic Development

_____	_____	Use of simple sentences (subject-verb)	
_____	_____	Use of compound subjects or verbs	
_____	_____	Use of compound sentences	
_____	_____	Use of passive voice	
_____	_____	Use of subordinate conjunctions	
_____	_____	Use of sentences with more than one dependent clause	
_____	_____	Sentence length	
_____	_____	Grammar	
_____	_____	Ability to repeat sentences	

Organization of Expression

_____	_____	Appropriateness	
_____	_____	Coherence	
_____	_____	Organized retelling of narrative: main characters, problem, events, sequence. If important, causality, outcome, and generalizations, moral or theme.	
_____	_____	Organized retelling of nonfiction: purpose, main points, order, cause and effect, comparison or contrast, conclusion	
_____	_____	Telling a story (as above)	
_____	_____	Explaining, describing, informing (as above)	

Oral Language Assessment

EVALUATION OF ORAL LANGUAGE RECEPTION

Some students may have difficulty in oral language expression yet do well in language reception. Others may be weak in both areas. Generally, receptive language comprehension is more advanced than expressive language. The listening comprehension section of the Graded Passages test can be used as one measure of oral language reception. Other informal assessment procedures for those with poor listening comprehension include giving directions to which the student responds physically. For example: "Put this book on the table." Oral commissions may be given in increasing levels of difficulty in terms of abstractness, number, and sequence of commands. *Put this book on the table* is concrete and consists of one command. *Point to the largest book* is more abstract. *Put the book on the table; next, turn off the lamp, and then bring me an eraser* is a command with three sequenced parts. How well a student performs is an indication of ability to comprehend spoken language. Following directions is difficult for those with receptive language problems. It may be useful to contrast the student's abilities in nonverbal areas such as drawing, painting, crafts, and similar activities with verbal performance. Also, arithmetic calculation abilities can be contrasted with arithmetic reasoning in story problems.

Some of the testing procedures listed under Oral Language and Cloze Tests may be used to evaluate receptive language abilities, but one should keep in mind that most require oral responses. Those who appear to have difficulties in oral language reception should be referred to specialists in communication disorders for more careful evaluation and, if necessary, language development. Of course, the need for an auditory acuity evaluation is also indicated to rule out hearing difficulties.

The Peabody Picture Vocabulary Test (Circle Pines, MN: American Guidance Service, 1997), may be quite useful in evaluating oral language reception of standard American English. The examiner should consider the student's background of experience and the demands of the test to determine whether it is appropriate.

WRITING EVALUATION

Handwriting: Writing Letters

Nonreaders or those on the beginning levels should be tested for their ability to write letters. The first phonics test, Letter Names, may be dictated to the student for this purpose. A complete inventory includes the ability to use manuscript letters in upper- and lowercase, and for more advanced students, the ability to write cursive letters in upper- and lowercase.

Handwriting: Writing Words in Sentences

Obtain a sample of the student's best effort. If one is not available, say, "I would like to see your best handwriting. Please write what I say." Give the student lined paper appropriate in spacing to his or her age. A graded passage on the student's independent reading level may be used for dictation. Older students may be given a graded passage to copy in cursive writing. Use the handwriting section of the Written Language Expression Checklist (p. 135) to evaluate the student's effort.

Near- and Far-Point Copying

Ask students to copy passages on their highest independent reading levels from a distance of 10 or 12 feet and from a copy on their desk in front of them. They should copy different passages of the same length and difficulty. The examiner should record the time taken to copy each passage and should observe the number of letters and words copied after each glance, pointing behavior, auditorizing, and other indicators of difficulty or ease with the task. A comparison of time and behaviors for the two tasks may reveal problems in near-point or far-point vision. Memory span for written language may also be evaluated.

Writing from Dictation

This task may be used to evaluate the student's ability to remember spoken words and phrases in a meaningful context. Students with problems in this area may be able to write only one or two words at a time. As the examiner dictates the passage, he or she should observe the student's accuracy and adjust the number of words dictated accordingly.

Expressing Ideas in Writing

Obtain samples of the student's best efforts to express ideas in writing. If these are not available, give the student a picture (as in the Oral Language Assessment procedure) and ask him or her to write a story about it. Using the same device for evaluating written and oral language gives the examiner an opportunity to compare development. Usually a student's oral expression is better, but some students with retrieval problems may do better in written expression. Give the student unlimited time to write, but note the time taken to produce the story.

Use the Written Language Expression Checklist to evaluate the student's efforts. The student's general development in writing can be evaluated by preparing a file of several writing samples typical of students in each grade level and comparing products.

Student's name _____ Date _____

WRITTEN LANGUAGE EXPRESSION: CHILDREN

Yes	No	Comparison with Peers Indicates Satisfactory Performance in:	Descriptions and Examples of Problems
____	____	Copying letters	_____
____	____	Writing letters from dictation	_____
____	____	Writing sentences from dictation	_____

Handwriting

Yes	No		
____	____	Letter formation	_____
____	____	Proportion slant	_____
____	____	Rate of letter production	_____
____	____	Spacing letters, words, lines	_____
____	____	Legibility	_____

Syntactic Development

Yes	No		
____	____	Writing complete sentences	_____
____	____	Writing sentences of appropriate length and complexity	_____
____	____	Using correct grammar	_____

Mechanics

Yes	No		
____	____	Using capital letters	_____
____	____	Using punctuation	_____

Level of Abstraction

Yes	No		
____	____	Ability to describe concrete objects and actions	_____
____	____	Ability to present and discuss ideas	_____

Organization and Presentation of Ideas

Yes	No		
____	____	Coherence within sentences, paragraphs, total story, or essay	_____
____	____	Using organizational patterns: narrative, expository, sequence, cause-effect, comparison, contrast	_____
____	____	Using appropriate vocabulary	_____
____	____	Proofreading and correcting	_____
____	____	Other observations	_____

_____
_____
_____

WRITING SCALE: ADULTS

Indicate +, yes or −, no

| Levels | Student's Name: _____ | Date: _____ |

0   Unable to write letters of the alphabet

1   Able to _____ write or _____ copy name.
Able to _____ write or _____ copy _____ part or _____ all of address.
Able to _____ write upper- and _____ lowercase letters.
Able to write words phonetically. _____

2   Able to write name and address. _____
Able to write simple sentences. _____
Able to use upper- and lowercase properly. _____
Able to spell _____ few _____ some _____ most words.

3   Able to write complex sentences. _____
Able to write in paragraphs. _____
Able to describe concrete objects and actions. _____
Able to use correct grammar _____ some or _____ most of the time.
Able to use correct punctuation _____ some or _____ most of the time.

4   Able to present and discuss ideas. _____
Able to write sentences of appropriate length and complexity. _____
Able to demonstrate coherence within and across paragraphs. _____
Able to use correct grammar. _____
Able to use correct punctuation. _____
Able to use appropriate vocabulary. _____
Able to write business letters. _____
Able to write for academic classes. _____

5   Able to write fluently. _____
Able to use organizational patterns: narrative _____, expository _____, sequence _____, cause and effect _____, comparison _____, contrast. _____
Able to fit writing styles to audience. _____
Able to proofread and correct writing. _____

Notes:

ARITHMETIC TEST

Purpose

An arithmetic test is included as a supplement to the battery for two reasons. First, the ability to perform basic arithmetic tasks is not dependent on reading. Students who do quite well in arithmetic, in contrast to reading, give evidence of their potential. The converse, of course, is not true. If a student does not do well in both reading and arithmetic, this does not mean potential is lacking but may indicate other underlying problems or simply a lack of instruction. Second, the writer of this test feels that remedial specialists and teachers should give assistance in all areas of essential needs such as reading, writing, spelling, and arithmetic. Overspecialization, leading to fragmentation in instruction, can result in an area of basic functioning being neglected.

Administration

Give the student the test page and scrap paper to use. Say, *"Please work as many of these problems as quickly as you can. Be careful, but try not to waste time."* Allow 5 minutes, exactly! The test may be continued untimed after the problems that were finished have been noted. Additional answers obtained after 5 minutes are not to be included in the scoring but can be used to obtain further information. Observe the student's work unobtrusively.

The test may be given untimed. The grade-level score is only an estimate. What is important is the student's ability to perform the operations.

Scoring and Interpretation

Total the number of right answers and refer to the answer key (p. 139) to obtain an estimate of level of performance. Note the categories of operations that the student understands. In addition, look for evidence of transposing or reversing numbers; consider whether the operation has been performed correctly even though the calculation was incorrect; look at rate in relation to accuracy; observe the student's need to verbalize; make tally marks; and so forth.

ARITHMETIC TEST

1. $\begin{array}{r} 3 \\ +4 \\ \hline \end{array}$

2. $\begin{array}{r} 5 \\ 3 \\ +4 \\ \hline \end{array}$

3. $\begin{array}{r} 7 \\ -3 \\ \hline \end{array}$

4. $\begin{array}{r} 12 \\ -5 \\ \hline \end{array}$

5. $\begin{array}{r} 761 \\ 543 \\ +123 \\ \hline \end{array}$

6. $\begin{array}{r} 592 \\ -363 \\ \hline \end{array}$

7. $\begin{array}{r} 7 \\ \times 3 \\ \hline \end{array}$

8. $\begin{array}{r} 402 \\ \times 9 \\ \hline \end{array}$

9. $4\overline{)24}$

10. $9\overline{)954}$

11. $5\overline{)46}$

12. $\begin{array}{r} 32 \\ \times 7 \\ \hline \end{array}$

13. $\begin{array}{r} 7291 \\ -5460 \\ \hline \end{array}$

14. $\begin{array}{r} 42 \\ \times 73 \\ \hline \end{array}$

15. $23\overline{)1081}$

16. $\begin{array}{r} 7 \\ +2\frac{1}{4} \\ \hline \end{array}$

17. $\begin{array}{r} \frac{1}{4} \\ +\frac{3}{8} \\ \hline \end{array}$

18. $\begin{array}{r} 5\frac{1}{2} \\ -3 \\ \hline \end{array}$

19. $\begin{array}{r} 7 \\ -4\frac{2}{3} \\ \hline \end{array}$

20. $\begin{array}{r} \frac{2}{3} \\ \frac{1}{2} \\ +\frac{1}{6} \\ \hline \end{array}$

21. $\begin{array}{r} 371\frac{3}{8} \\ +17\frac{1}{4} \\ \hline \end{array}$

22. $\begin{array}{r} 16 \\ \times 3\frac{1}{4} \\ \hline \end{array}$

23. $\frac{3}{4} \times \frac{2}{5} =$

24. $\frac{3}{4} \div \frac{1}{2} =$

25. $\begin{array}{r} 37 \\ \times .04 \\ \hline \end{array}$

26. $\begin{array}{r} .42 \\ .01 \\ +3.713 \\ \hline \end{array}$

27. $7\overline{)4.41}$

28. $.07\overline{)21.63}$

29. $\begin{array}{r} 29.1 \\ \times 4.54 \\ \hline \end{array}$

30. Write $\frac{1}{4}$ as a decimal ____

ARITHMETIC TEST ANSWER KEY

1. 7	6. 229	11. 9.2	16. $9\frac{1}{4}$	21. $388\frac{5}{8}$	26. 4.143
2. 12	7. 21	12. 224	17. $\frac{5}{8}$	22. 52	27. .63
3. 4	8. 3618	13. 1831	18. $2\frac{1}{2}$	23. $\frac{3}{10}$	28. 309
4. 7	9. 6	14. 3066	19. $2\frac{1}{3}$	24. $1\frac{1}{2}$	29. 132.114
5. 1427	10. 106	15. 47	20. $\frac{8}{6}$ or $1\frac{1}{3}$	25. 1.48	30. .25

Raw Score (Number Right) and Grade Equivalent

Score	0	1	2	3	4	5	6	7	8	9	10	11	12
Grade	1.0	1.5	2.0	2.5	3.0	3.5	3.8	4.0	4.3	4.5	4.8	5.0	5.3

Score	13	14	15	16	17	18	19	20	21	22	23	24	25+
Grade	5.5	5.8	6.3	6.5	7.0	7.5	8.0	8.5	9.0	9.5	10.0	10.5	10.5+

Calculation Categories

simple addition: 1, 2, 5
addition of fractions: 16, 17, 20, 21
addition of decimals: 26
simple subtraction: 3, 4, 6, 13
subtraction of fractions: 18, 19
simple multiplication: 7, 8, 12, 14

multiplication of fractions: 22, 23
multiplication of decimals: 25, 29
simple division: 9, 10, 11, 15
division of fractions: 24
division of decimals: 27, 28
decimal conversion: 30

Arithmetic Test

OPEN-BOOK READING ASSESSMENTS

Description

Open-book reading assessments (OBRAs) are informal silent reading assessments employing questions to be answered or tasks to be performed by the reader with the selection provided. The material is taken from academic material or daily-life reading. The skills tested by questions or tasks may reflect course goals or life competencies. OBRAs are most appropriate for those reading above the third-grade level. They may be used with individuals or with groups.

Purposes

The purposes of the open-book tests are (1) to obtain specific information on students' abilities to understand and use content area, vocational, or daily-life reading materials; (2) to plan instruction; and (3) to confirm or supplement other diagnostic data.

Construction

1. Portions of material considered to be typical reading for the student within particular areas of emphasis should be selected. For content areas this might include textbooks, periodicals, or pamphlets; for vocational areas, manuals, indexes, or directories; and for other life-role areas, newspapers, schedules, and catalogs. Passage length will depend on the student's reading ability.

2. To determine the abilities to be evaluated, consider (a) the nature of the tasks to be performed with the material and the levels of comprehension required and (b) the enabling skills required to perform the tasks or comprehend the information. With regard to tasks and levels, will the reader need to interpret graphs and maps? Follow directions? Identify summarizing or main-idea statements? Evaluate information? When the main objectives of using the material have been determined, the test constructor can then turn to the enabling objectives. For example, will the reader be able to understand the technical and general vocabulary? Skim to find specific items of information? To perceive the organization of the information?

3. Multiple choice, matching, or short-answer test items should be constructed. These will be easier to score, but, more importantly, they will evaluate the student's ability to understand what was read rather than the ability to express one-self (a higher level of functioning). This is not to say that expression should not be tested but that the underlying ability, comprehension, should be tested separately. In this way, the diagnostician can separate those students who comprehend but cannot express themselves verbally from those who cannot comprehend *and* cannot express themselves verbally.

4. Page and paragraph numbers should be provided for each question unless surveying or locational skills are being tested. The more items within a category, the more reliable the test. At least five or six items per category should be constructed. The test should be piloted on a sample of average readers, and poor items should be rewritten or discarded.

5. Separate writing assessments may evaluate the ability to summarize, to evaluate, and to relate information.

Sample categories and questions from various content areas:

Technical Vocabulary

1. fossil (page 230, paragraph 2)
    (a) A rock shaped by wind or water into the form of an animal
    (b) A trace of an animal or plant that lived long ago
    (c) A search for animals that lived in the Ice Age
    (d) A plan to reconstruct animals from the Ice Age
    (e) I don't know

2. composing room (page 22, paragraph 1)
    (a) Where news is set in type
    (b) Where news articles are written
    (c) Where news items are selected
    (d) Where news policy is established
    (e) I don't know

General Vocabulary

1. distinguish (page 50, paragraph 5)
    (a) Group together
    (b) Give a name
    (c) Tell apart
    (d) Find a total
    (e) I don't know

2. dwells (page 6, paragraph 6)
    (a) Eats
    (b) Dives
    (c) Walks
    (d) Lives
    (e) I don't know

Specific Context Clues to Vocabulary

1. coagulates (page 42). The acid thickens or *coagulates* the proteins of milk.
    (a) Makes a larger quantity
    (b) Makes more dense
    (c) Makes more digestible
    (d) Makes sour tasting
    (e) I don't know

2. opaque (page 40). You can see through glass, but wood is *opaque*.
    (a) Can't be melted
    (b) Can't break it
    (c) Can't be bent
    (d) Can't look through it
    (e) I don't know

Main Ideas

1. The main idea (important principle) on page 22 is
    (a) Winds blow across the water.
    (b) Evaporation lowers the air temperature.
    (c) Moisture is removed from the air.
    (d) Refrigerators can help preserve food.
    (c) I don't know

2. The main idea (statement of theory) on page 108 is:
   (a) The United States is in the temperate zone.
   (b) Countries in temperate zones make greater progress.
   (c) Progress is measured by gross national product.
   (d) Climate affects the course of world history.
   (e) I don't know

Literal Details
1. Circle three examples of an amphibian (pages 29 and 30)
   (a) frog
   (b) bird
   (c) fish
   (d) turtle
   (e) toad
   (f) alligator
   (g) salamander
   (h) water buffalo
   (i) snake
2. The new stars of 1600 and 1604 were observed by (page 32)
   (a) Galileo
   (b) Copernicus
   (c) Kepler
   (d) Tycho Brahe
   (e) I don't know

Interpretation
1. Match the following statements to the diagrams:

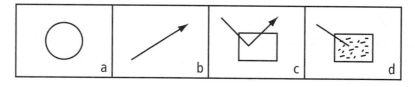

   _____ Light can be bent. (p. 40)
   _____ Light can be reflected. (p. 41)
   _____ Light travels in straight lines. (p. 40)
   _____ Light can be absorbed. (p. 42)
   _____ Light can travel through space. (p. 42)
2. Sam's mother appeared to be (pp. 80–82)
   (a) worried
   (b) disappointed
   (c) angry
   (d) pleased about his new job
   (e) not concerned

Using Charts
1. Olefin is cleaned by (p. 57)
   (a) Washing in warm water
   (b) Washing in hot water
   (c) Dry cleaning
   (d) Brushing with cornstarch
   (e) I don't know

2. The distance from Lansing to Central City is (see map grid)
   - (a) 62 miles
   - (b) 72 miles
   - (c) 86 miles
   - (d) 59 miles
   - (e) I don't know

Using Book Parts

In my textbook, to find quickly	I would turn to:	on page:
_____ _____ A definition of a technical word	(a) table of contents	(1) ii
_____ _____ Pages that mention a particular person's name	(b) the glossary	(2) 390
_____ _____ A statement of why the author wrote the book	(c) preface	(3) iii
_____ _____ Name of book's publisher	(d) title page	(4) vii
_____ _____ Outline of what is in the book	(e) index	(5) 385

Administration

Students should be given a generous amount of time, although those who take much longer than others should be noted as they may require further testing. The OBRA may be given in sections so that students who are unable to concentrate for a sustained period will not be inclined to guess or mark answers without reading the material. As with all test administration, students should be given clear, explicit instructions, encouraged to do their best, and observed for evidence of inattention to the task or confusion over test directions.

Scoring

As a general guide, 80% may be considered adequate for most categories. If several students are tested, the results might be charted as follows:

	Literal Details						Technical Vocabulary						Main Ideas						And so on
	1	2	3	4	5	6	7	8	9	10	11	12	13	14	15	16	17	18	
Jim	x	x		x	x		x	x		x	x	x			x		x		
Sue	x	x	x	x	x	x	x	x	x	x	x		x						
Donald	x	x		x						x	x						x		
Linda	x	x	x	x	x	x	x	x	x	x	x	x	x	x	x		x	x	
And so on																			

Note: The number refers to the test item; an "x" indicates a correct answer.

Analysis

An analysis of the results can provide information on specific strengths and weaknesses. If the chart is read vertically, it can reveal group needs; if read horizontally, it can indicate individual needs. Jim, for example, needs help in identifying main ideas in his textbooks, whereas Donald's low performance in one of the easier sections of the test, literal comprehension, suggests the need for further evaluation in the areas of general vocabulary and underlying concepts. If these are quite low, he should not be required to use this text. If these are satisfactory, Donald's listening comprehension of the material should be evaluated to see whether he can have the textbook read to him while instruction is provided to improve his technical vocabulary and comprehension.

Students should be given feedback on their performance. This can be done by photocopying the chart, cutting it into strips, and giving each student his or her results. Then the teacher can explain the reasoning processes and knowledge required by each category. This might be the first time some of the students have gotten any insights as to what their comprehension skills are and what kinds of reasoning need to be done to comprehend various kinds of printed matter.

The OBRA can be extended over grade levels by constructing additional tests for material on higher and lower grade levels. Donald might be evaluated on easier material, whereas Linda might be evaluated on more challenging material. Students have a level at which they can function fairly well, but within that level they have strengths and weaknesses.

The teacher can develop a file of OBRAs on materials on different levels in various areas over a period of time that can be used to supplement a diagnostic battery or to place students in materials.

PART THREE

Recording, Summarizing,
Interpreting

BACKGROUND INFORMATION: K–12

Classroom Teacher's Referral Information

Student: _____

Teacher: _____

Grade: _____
    Year   Month

Age: __ _____
    Year   Month

1. Student's reading level: _____

2. Title of reading text or program: _____ Level: _____
   Supplementary material most frequently used

   Title: _____ Level: _____

   Title: _____ Level: _____

3. Reading abilities

   Word Identification

Strengths	Needs		Comments
_____	_____	Beginning consonants	_____
_____	_____	Ending consonants	_____
_____	_____	Long vowels	_____
_____	_____	Fluency	_____
_____	_____	Short vowels	_____
_____	_____	Letter combinations	_____
_____	_____	Use of letter-sound knowledge	_____
_____	_____	Sight vocabulary	_____
_____	_____	Recognition of compound words	_____
_____	_____	Recognition of multisyllable words	_____

   Comprehension

Strengths	Needs		Comments
_____	_____	Activates background knowledge	_____
_____	_____	Predicts	_____
_____	_____	Understands major concepts	_____
_____	_____	Self-monitors	_____
_____	_____	Recalls with prompts	_____
_____	_____	Recalls without prompts	_____
_____	_____	Interprets meaning suggested by the text	_____

Continued

4. Reading abilities

Strengths	Weaknesses		Comments
_____	_____ Spelling		_____
_____	_____ Handwriting		_____
_____	_____ Listening comprehension		_____
_____	_____ Study skills		_____
_____	_____ Oral expression		_____
_____	_____ Mathematics		_____
_____	_____ Written expression		_____

5. Has student received special help in reading? _____ When? _____

   Nature of instruction? _____

   Results? _____

   _____

6. Attitudes

Strengths	Needs		Comments
_____	_____ Ability to concentrate		_____
_____	_____ Confidence in ability		_____
_____	_____ Willing to risk error		_____
_____	_____ Intent to remember		_____
_____	_____ Ability to work alone		_____
_____	_____ Enjoyment of material read aloud		_____

7. Interests _____

   School _____

   After school _____

   Favorite books _____

8. Health

Strengths	Needs		Nature of problem(s), if any
_____	_____ Vision		_____
_____	_____ Hearing		_____
_____	_____ Other		_____

9. Student strengths _____

10. Student needs (other than reading) _____

11. Additional information you feel is important _____

_____

CHILD'S HOME INFORMATION

Child's name: _____ Birth Date: _____

Address: _____ Phone: _____

Language(s) spoken in home: _____

Childhood diseases, serious injuries, surgery, and age at which each occurred: _____

_____

Does your child wear, or has she or he ever worn, glasses? _____

    If so, why? _____

When was your child's last vision check? _____

    Results? _____

Has your child had many ear infections? _____

Has your child's hearing been examined by a doctor? _____

Do you think your child hears well? _____

Does your child have any health problems? Explain. _____

When was your child last examined by a physician? _____

List any types of medication your child is now receiving. _____

Do you feel your child has any speech or language problems? _____

    If so, describe. _____

Do you think your child misses too much school? _____

    Has your child ever missed school for long periods of time? If so, explain. _____

    _____

What is your child's attitude toward school? _____

What are his or her best subjects? _____ Worse subjects? _____

What is your child's attitude toward reading? _____

When was his or her difficulty with reading first noticed? _____

What do you think may be the cause of your child's reading problems? _____

Does your child read voluntarily? _____ What? _____

Are there reading materials in your home that are appropriate for your child? _____

Does your child spend time on schoolwork at home? _____

Does your child have a quiet place to study? _____

Is there anyone at home who can help him or her to read? _____

How much time does your child spend watching television? _____

Continued

How does your child get along with siblings? _____

    Others his or her age? _____ Parents? _____

What is his or her usual disposition? _____

Do you think your child gets enough rest? _____

    Does she or he become easily fatigued? _____

Does your child generally listen attentively when you talk to him or her? _____

Does your child follow directions well? _____

Does your child generally see tasks through to completion? _____

How does your child usually react to authority? _____

Are there situations in which your child becomes easily frustrated? _____

    If so, explain. _____

Please add any information that you feel will aid in understanding and helping your child. Include strengths and interests.

_____

_____

Name of person completing form: _____

Relationship to child: _____

K–12 SUMMARY

BADER Reading and Language Inventory

Student's name: _____ School: _____ Date: _____

Grade in school: _____ Age: _____ Birth Date: _____ Examiner: _____

I. Reading Profile

Language development: Low _____ Average _____ High _____

English language learner: No _____ Yes _____   Level: _____

    Recommended level for instruction _____

    Recommended level for independent learning:

    ___ Word list

    ___ Oral reading

    ___ Silent reading comprehension

    ___ Listening comprehension

Instructional Needs in Reading

Word Recognition	*Comprehension*
___ Semantic cues	___ Prior knowledge
___ Syntactic cues	___ Prediction strategies
___ Grapho-phonic cues	___ Self-monitoring
___ Consonant sounds	___ Literal
___ Vowel sounds	___ Interpretive
___ Blending	___ Narrative
___ Structural analysis	___ Expository
___ Automaticity	___ Vocabulary
	___ Rate

II. Language Development Needs

___ Receptive language	___ Written expression
___ English language learner	___ Conceptual development
___ Oral expression	___ Vocabulary development

Continued

III. Other Instructional Needs

____ Spelling ____ Handwriting ____ Arithmetic

IV. Visual-Auditory Difficulties

___ Visual acuity   ____ Auditory acuity

___ Visual discrimination   ____ Auditory discrimination

V. Preliteracy

___ Language awareness   ____ Hearing letters and sounds in words

___ Blending   ____ Matching words in sentences

___ Segmenting   ____ Comprehending stories

___ Letter knowledge

VI. Student Strengths

_____

_____

VII. Student Priorities, Interests, Concerns

_____

_____

VIII. Summary of Recommendations for Instruction

_____

_____

_____

_____

_____

_____

_____

_____

INSTRUCTOR'S RECORDS: K–12

A separate folder, in addition to a portfolio, may be kept by the instructor for each student so that a summary of progress is readily at hand. This information is essential for evaluating programs or reporting to administrators, funding agencies, parents, or other schools or instructors. Student confidentiality must be respected. Record folders should be kept in a secure location.

Depending on the age and literacy level of the student, the instructor's folder may include the initial intake information, student goals and interests, test results, and some of the following dated items administered or completed at appropriate intervals:

Reading level, derived from the word list and passages.

Reading conferences chart indicating title, type of text, level of text, student's skill in word analysis, vocabulary knowledge, fluency, literal, inferential, applied critical reading, and other responses.

Open-book reading assessment summaries, based on academic, workplace, business, or personal needs reading.

Writing samples from in-class work on personal, narrative, expository, academic, workplace, business, or life-role needs.

Writing conferences chart indicating type of writing, strengths, needs in content, style, cohesiveness, organization, grammar, mechanics, and spelling.

Record of student progress toward goals or standards.

Notes on review of student portfolio.

Results of student and teacher conferences on progress and future plans.

ADULT INTAKE INFORMATION

Name: _____ Phone: _____ Best hours: _____

Address: _____

_____ Okay to leave messages? Yes _____ No _____

Person providing information: _____

Relationship to prospective student: _____

Does student know you are calling us? Yes _____ No _____

Program to respond: ABE _____ Independent _____ Other _____

Interview

1. Interests/hobbies:

2. Family concerns:

3. Employment:

4. Education:

5. Current reading skills (What things are easy to read or write? What things are hard to read or write? How are your math skills?):

6. Health problems related to learning:

   _____ Vision _____ Speech _____ Hearing _____ Other

7. Language facility (ELL? Articulate? Fluent?):

8. Other observations:

Matching Information

Days available: _____

_____

Times available: Day _____ and Evening _____

Geographical preference

City: _____ N ___ S ___ W ___ E ___

Near home:

Flexible:

Have tutoring site to suggest:

Other:

Have transportation? Yes ___ No ___

Notes:

ADULT-LEVEL SUMMARY
BADER Reading and Language Inventory

Student's name: _____ Staff: _____ Date: _____

1. Reading level: _____ (word list: _____ passages: _____)

2. Language comprehension: appears low _____ , average _____ , high _____ , ELL _____

3. Instructional needs:

_____ Alphabet	_____ Multisyllabic words
_____ Name	_____ Vocabulary
_____ Write	_____ Spelling*
_____ Sight words	_____ Rate/fluency
_____ Consonant sounds	_____ Writing
_____ Vowel patterns	_____ Study skills
_____ Letter combinations	_____ Math
_____ Use of context	_____ Other _____
_____ Use of phonics	

Sight words recognized (primer level and below; experience list): _____

_____

4. Student strengths: _____

_____

5. Student goals, interests, concerns: _____

_____

_____

6. Suggestions for materials or methods: _____

_____

_____

_____

_____

_____

_____

THE ADULT LIFE-ROLE PORTFOLIO

Adult literacy tutors may adapt ideas from this section to keep a record of student goals, interests, and needs. After discussion with each student to determine the portfolio purposes, write the purposes as the student dictates them; then discuss the organization of the portfolio, where it will be kept, who will have access to it, how it will be used, and other concerns of the student to her or his satisfaction. Purposes and plans may be adjusted over time.

A suggested way to organize the portfolio is to have sections on:

Reading for enjoyment and information.* The student may keep a log of articles and books, as in this example:

Date	Title	New Ideas/Words	Comments

Tapes of student's reading may be made to demonstrate growth. The student can also be helped to make a list of topics and specific titles of books and magazines for future reading.

Document reading and writing.* The teacher and student collect materials basic to daily life needs and interests, such as:

Transportation: road signs; bus, train, subway signs; destinations on vehicles; maps, schedules; driver's manuals

Food: package labels, directions for preparation, recipes, menus

Health: directions on prescriptions and over-the-counter items, directions for follow-up, home medical care, infant and child care, health history forms

Workplace: want ads, job applications, memos from supervisors, simple computer entries, time slips, performance indicators, job outlines, agreements

Safety: danger and warning signs, instructions to operate appliances and equipment

Assistance and information: telephone book, newspaper, directories

The student chooses the items he or she wants to master and prioritizes them for study with the teacher's help. Lists may be kept of words to learn to read and write for each item. A log may be kept of documents mastered. A copy of the most important, correctly completed forms should be given to the student for his or her use.

Quantitative reading and writing.* Procedures are followed as in the preceding section. Materials may include bills, checks, bank statements, loan agreements, rental agreements, warranties, guarantees, tax forms, advertisements, social security forms, price tags, order forms, and refund and discount information.

Personal, business, and creative writing. The student chooses the kinds of writing most important to him or her: letters and notes to friends, family, child's teacher; an autobiography; letters requesting information or assistance; letters to the editor; poems, stories, essays, scripts, journals, ideas for future projects, photo album notations, baby books.

Oral and nonverbal language. The student chooses areas of importance: polite social and business greetings and exchanges, giving and receiving directions, explaining, requesting, imagining. Evidence of growth may be documented by tapes, checklists, and anecdotal reports.

Student self-evaluations. Based on her or his goals, the student selects areas to evaluate and notes progress with the teacher's help. Take care to examine only one or two elements at a time and celebrate achievements.

*Note: Please attach spelling paper to back of this form.

USING STANDARDS DOCUMENTS IN PORTFOLIOS

Portfolio contents may be used to demonstrate achievement of district, state, or national standards and goals. For example, a student's reading log may help meet the standard of "reading a variety of genres for enjoyment." A student's social studies report may help meet the standard of "synthesizing information from several sources." State departments of education and school districts have developed goal standards and benchmark documents that may be obtained for adoption or adaptation.

Recommended Reading

NAEP Reading Consensus Project. (1992). *Reading framework for the 1992 national assessment of educational progress.* Washington, DC: U.S. Government Printing Office.

Tierney, R. J., Carter, M. A., & Desai, L. E. (1991). *Portfolio assessment in the reading and writing classroom.* Norwood, VA: Christopher Gordon Publishers.

Wolf, D. P. (1989). Portfolio assessment: Sample student work. *Educational Leadership, 46,* 35–39.

Yancy, K. B. (Ed.). (1992). *Portfolios in the writing classroom.* Champaign, IL: National Council of Teachers of English.

*Areas selected for evaluation of literacy in the 1992 National Adult Literacy Survey sponsored by the U.S. Department of Education.

CASE STUDY: JACKIE

Michelle Johnston, Dean, College of Education, Ferris University, presents the following case study to illustrate the reasoning of a reading diagnostician as he uses the BADER *Reading and Language Inventory to assess a child's reading needs and make recommendations for instruction.*

GETTING STARTED

Ms. Irving referred Jackie to the school district reading diagnostician during March of second grade. When Mr. Frank, the diagnostician, reviewed Ms. Irving's reasons for referring Jackie for a reading diagnosis (see Classroom Teacher's Referral Information form, p. 147), examined her cumulative records, observed her classroom performance, and interviewed her mother (see Child's Home Information form, p. 149), he discovered that her reading difficulties were not new. In fact, Jackie had a history of delayed language acquisition, apparent difficulties learning various reading conventions in kindergarten and first grade, and comprehension problems. However, according to her mother; her current teacher, Ms. Irving; and her previous teacher; her reading difficulties did not appear very severe earlier. But as the reading materials became more complex, she exhibited increasing levels of difficulty and frustration. Mr. Frank also found that Jackie moved twice in kindergarten and once near the end of first grade in addition to missing a significant amount of second grade. She has attended Wilson Elementary since late April of first grade. Her first-grade teacher noted some difficulties, but indicated that she really did not have time to investigate those difficulties in late May and June.

HOME AND FAMILY RESOURCES

Jackie's mother was concerned about her reading progress, but as a single parent who worked evenings and supported three other children without financial assistance, she did not have time to work with Jackie. Her mother reported that a grandmother helped with babysitting and child care, but there really were not extra resources in the family to afford many books or programs such as summer reading programs between first and second grades or, looking ahead, between second and third. However, she was willing to figure out some at-home tutoring program and thought that the grandmother or a cousin could help.

RULING OUT PROBLEMS AND DEVELOPING A DIAGNOSTIC PLAN

Because Mr. Frank was concerned about Jackie's reported language delay and difficulty learning reading conventions, including phonics, he decided to rule out any physical issues that would interfere with her reading progress. Therefore, with the help of the school nurse and speech/language consultant, he recommended thorough vision, hearing, and language screenings. While he waited for the results of the screenings, Mr. Frank met with Jackie and began the BADER Reading and Language Inventory with an interview using the Student Priorities and Interests form. He found her to be energetic and positive, but aware that she was not reading as well as the other students in her class. Although Jackie liked listening to stories and reading predictable books, she appeared to be embarrassed about her reading and lacked confidence. In making decisions about his diagnostic strategies, Mr. Frank integrated the research findings from Snow et al. (1998) regarding preventing reading difficulties with the BADER Reading and Language Inventory to formulate his diagnostic plan (see Flowcharts). Specifically, he determined that once he knew her reading level he also would rule out the following difficulties:

phonemic awareness; motor development; letter identification; automaticity; visual, verbal, and aural processing; and language development. Therefore, he started with the Preprimer (PP) word list and found her instructional level using the word lists to be at the primer (P) level.

By the time Mr. Frank completed Jackie's interview and presented the word lists to her, the nurse and speech/language consultant were ready to share their findings. Jackie's vision and hearing were normal; however, the speech/language consultant felt that her oral language was somewhat low for her age level. She was especially concerned about her vocabulary development. Therefore, she went beyond her usual work with Jackie and investigated her understanding of concepts, where, again, Jackie appeared to be performing slightly below most children her age. From the conference with the other two specialists, Mr. Frank began formulating Jackie's reading profile with the following observations: He would recommend that the speech/language consultant work with Ms. Irving to select activities to improve Jackie's concept and vocabulary/language development.

ANALYZING READING ABILITIES

Using her performance on the word lists as a guide, Mr. Frank invited Jackie to begin reading the oral paragraphs at the primer level. Her oral reading performance, including accuracy and recall, was the first-grade level. However, she read deliberately, word by word. She did recognize punctuation and exhibited unaided recall of the information at the literal level. When she did not know a word, she did not attempt to decode or identify the word through context clues. Therefore, the unknown words interfered with her ability to read orally and understand the passages. When Mr. Frank asked her to read silently, she whispered the words in the passage and did not read silently. Mr. Frank noted that Jackie's listening comprehension was on the second-grade level. He added the following information to Jackie's reading profile to share with Ms. Irving and her mother:

Recommended level for instruction, first grade; independent reading level, primer; listening comprehension, second grade; comprehension appeared to be literal, not interpretive

Mr. Frank was optimistic because Jackie could listen to second-grade-level passages and understand them. He told her mother and teacher that her listening comprehension indicated that she could make progress once he figured out the difficulties that were impeding her progress. He recommended that they read to her, talk about the stories they were reading, have her read to them, and start finding interesting words in the stories and environment to discuss. To move her comprehension to an interpretive level, he encouraged them to have her create different story endings, ask "why" questions, and think about "what if" scenarios with the stories that they read. Additionally, he asked Jackie to start writing a journal to record interesting ideas from stories and words that she either saw or heard spoken to share with others.

Mr. Frank also suggested that her mother and teacher read in unison with her and that her teacher include choral reading as a reading instructional activity. Through reading in unison and choral reading, Jackie could develop fluency and eventually read more smoothly. Spending some time independently reading high-interest books on the primer level would contribute to instant word recognition, fluency, and enjoyment of reading. Jackie liked to read about animals, particularly cats. Easy-to-read books about cats were readily available.

FINDING SPECIFIC NEEDS

Before Mr. Frank gave Jackie the Diagnostic Spelling tests, he asked Jackie to bring samples of her writing to the next session and requested that Ms. Irving also share Jackie's writing samples. He was interested in finding patterns of errors that would give him clues about Jackie's phonetic and visual acuity. After analyzing her performance on the Diagnostic Spelling test, Mr. Frank determined that Jackie's estimated performance was on the preprimer level. She seemed to recognize beginning and ending sounds represented by single consonants in words, but had difficulty with middle sounds; she rarely made substitutions. Therefore, he decided to use the Visual Discrimination tests and Auditory Discrimination test in the Preliteracy Testing Record to get to the underlying problem.

Remarkably, Jackie did very well on the Visual Discrimination tests, ruling out visual discrimination problems that interfered with her reading progress. However, her performance on the Auditory Discrimination test was problematic, indicating the need for additional assessment of her phonemic awareness and knowledge of phonics. Mr. Frank moved the diagnosis forward, skipping Literacy Concepts, because he knew that Jackie had a good understanding of the concepts, to the other subtests examining phonic elements. He omitted consonant testing, because she demonstrated knowledge in her spelling test. He found that she did not know many of the vowel sounds and had difficulty with blending and segmenting. Jackie demonstrated that her use of syntactic and semantic cues were appropriate for her age. Language processing did not appear to be a problem.

SUMMARIZING THE FINDINGS; MAKING RECOMMENDATIONS

After pinpointing some issues related to phonemic manipulation and phonics, Mr. Frank felt that he was prepared to complete his summary of Jackie's instructional needs. Although he was uncertain of the causes for her reading difficulties, he made several conjectures. He thought that her moving in kindergarten and first grade might have interfered with her progress. Perhaps the school districts were not consistent in their teaching of reading fundamentals or Jackie's own adjustment to the new schools was problematic. Mr. Frank also thought Jackie probably did not practice reading enough to habituate it. Therefore, his summary of her instructional needs included (1) ensuring that Jackie has lots of practice reading high-interest books; (2) developing competencies using grapho-phonic cues, segmenting, and blending by integrating oral language, reading, and writing activities; (3) engaging prior knowledge and prediction strategies to develop her self-monitoring capabilities; (4) exposing her to varieties of texts in different genre that would enhance her interpretive comprehension; (5) expanding her vocabulary (word meaning) through concept development; (6) building a repertoire of fix-up strategies to use when she encounters unknown words; and (7) embedding phonics instruction in context and in spelling.

Because Jackie is at the end of second grade, Mr. Frank found a tutor for her as well as a free summer program with trained teachers or tutors, from Volunteers In Service To America (VISTA) or America Reads. A senior citizen volunteer tutor contacted by Mr. Frank as well as a neighbor of Jackie's family offered to work with her twice a week and walk her to the library. Mr. Frank felt that Jackie could make good progress if this intensive help could continue through third grade.

CASE ANALYSIS

Many children like Jackie, who move frequently in their early schooling, miss the fundamentals of beginning reading instruction. Additionally, without access to children's books and sufficient practice reading, they do not habituate reading and develop fluency. Because Jackie was at the end of second grade, Ms. Irving and Mr. Frank had a daunting task. They had to ensure that she would enter third grade reading and writing successfully. According to Snow et al. (1998), when children do not learn to read by third grade, reading problems tend to plague them throughout their schooling because, in third grade and beyond, the focus moves from learning to read to reading to learn.

Mr. Frank provides a good example of a reading diagnostician by following organized diagnostic procedures. First, he ruled out vision, hearing, and language problems by seeking expert consultation and assistance as well as gaining a thorough understanding of Jackie's reading problems by checking records and interviewing her teachers and parent. Second, Mr. Frank formulated his plan based on sound theory and research. Third, as he gained information about Jackie, he shared it with the teacher and her mother, making recommendations for correction as he progressed through the diagnosis. Fourth, he combined samples of classroom work in spelling and writing with testing and skipped diagnosis subtests on which he knew she could succeed.

Ms. Irving was fortunate to have access to someone like Mr. Frank. However, if there were no reading diagnosticians available through her school district, Ms. Irving could have completed the BADER and Language Inventory as part of a classroom assessment strategy, making observations and giving subtests over a couple of weeks. Although in-depth testing takes time, there are usually only a few children in each classroom that need such a close look. With an understanding of their strengths and needs, they can succeed.

Snow, C. E., Burns, M. S., & Griffin, P. (Eds.). (1998). *Preventing reading difficulties in young children.* Washington, DC: National Academy Press. Available online: http://www.books.nap.edu/html/prdyc/

REFERRALS: CASE EXCERPTS

The primary purposes of an assessment are to discover students' interests and priorities and determine levels of literacy functioning, strengths, and instructional needs, but it is essential to be alert to physical, experiential, and emotional factors that may impact a student's learning. The following excerpts from case studies give examples of patterns of behavior that indicate the need to make referrals or consult with other professionals. Often, a student's struggle with reading causes stress resulting in negative behavior so that finding the underlying difficulty is challenging.

Vision: Juan, 10 years old; 4th grade; retained 1 year; reading level: 2nd grade

Inventory spelling tests and classroom writing samples revealed Juan's heavy dependence on phonetic spelling. His visual memory of words with silent letters was very poor. The visual discrimination task took Juan four and a half minutes to complete. He laboriously made comparisons, letter by letter, by using index fingers of both hands to make a match. When he was given the near- and far-point copying tasks on first-grade material, he took four minutes to copy from the board and eleven minutes to copy from the paper on his desk. When he copied from the board, he copied in phrases. His near-point copying was word by word. His head was close to the paper. A vision specialist confirmed Juan's near-point vision difficulty.

Hearing: Mai, 43 years old; adult basic education; reading level: 3rd grade

In her interview, Mai's articulation was indistinct. She pronounced *much* as *mush* and *yes* as *yesh*. Her spelling revealed the same pattern. *Mouth* was written as *moush*. Given the Auditory Discrimination of Word Pairs test, Mai missed 20 of 30 pairs. Audiometric testing revealed a severe, high-frequency hearing loss in both ears.

Language Expression: Mark: 9 years old; 4th grade; reading level: 2nd grade

Mark was teased, called stupid, and was told he "talked baby talk." In the Unfinished Sentences task he said, "I don't know how I got a new bike; next summer I gettin one." During oral passage reading, he read, "You can came home with me." His performance on the Grammatical Closure test indicated a lack of mastery of several grammatical forms. A sample of his conversation was taped and analyzed to confirm specific areas of difficulty. Mark was referred to the university auditory, speech, and language clinic. At the end of eight months his language expression was satisfactory.

Auditory Processing: Tyrone; 10th grade; reading level: high school

Some of Tyrone's teachers accused him of playing dumb and daydreaming. One teacher felt he had a hearing loss. He was earning As and Bs in science, but he was failing English and history. Tyrone's science teacher wrote instructions on the marking board and read them to the class. He didn't give lectures or lengthy oral directions as Tyrone's other teachers did. His students usually worked on papers at their desks.

In his interview, Tyrone was friendly. He had noticeable pauses before responding and gave brief answers. Tyrone read at the high school level with regard to pronouncing words, but he struggled in retelling and in responding to questions. When he was given an alternative passage with questions in writing and was allowed to respond in writing, he did well. He easily passed the Auditory Discrimination test.

A speech/language specialist confirmed Tyrone's difficulty with auditory processing. She explained his instructional needs to the staff, and helped Tyrone learn coping skills.

English Language Learning: Iwen: 3rd grade; reading level: 3rd grade

Iwen, whose first language was Malay, had difficulty spelling English words. She wrote *stan* for *stand*, *caldren* for *children*, and *smil* for *smile*. An adult Malay and English speaker explained that Malay words do not have an -nd ending so Iwen did not see the need to use *d* after *n* in *stand*. The letter *c* in the Malay language has the same sound as *ch*, which explains the omission of *h* in *children*. Malay also does not use a silent *e* at the end of words. Consultation with an appropriate bilingual speaker can be helpful to understand language differences that may impede literacy in English.

PART FOUR

Development of the Inventory: Validity and Reliability

PART FOUR

DEVELOPING AND VALIDATING
THE INVENTORY

The selection and development of the tasks in the inventory are based on several years' experience in individual assessment of elementary, secondary, and adult learners and on the basis of a careful analysis of research and authoritative opinion in the literature. All parts of the battery have been tested with the aid of experienced reading specialists on K–12 and adult levels with at least a master's degree in reading. Since the publication of the first edition, professors with doctorates in reading, special education, and speech and language have used the battery in preparing teachers and reading and language specialists, and endorsed its content and procedures. Fitzgerald (2001) explained in *Reading Research Quarterly* that she used the *BADER Reading and Language Inventory* in her study "because grade-level equivalents of passages of the published inventory are well established and because, unlike some other inventories, early reading levels are represented in both preprimer and primer passages, providing greater sensitivity to initial reading levels."

THE GRADED WORD LISTS

One purpose of the graded word list is to determine entry level for the graded passages. Words were selected from graded sight-word lists and readers that appeared to be appropriate for each level. The graded word list was tested by having reading specialists record the instructional level at which they had placed their students with mild to severe difficulties after diagnosis and trial teaching. Dr. Lonnie McIntyre, University of Tennessee, compared students' scores on the Bader word list and the Slosson Oral Reading Test and found a correlation of 9.2. Similar results were found by Dr. Janet Dynak, Western Michigan University.

THE GRADED READER'S PASSAGES

The graded passages were either written by the author or selected from materials that appeared to be typical for the grade-level designations. Research and experience indicate that performance is affected by the reader's attitude toward the content; therefore, passages were written or adapted that would be suitable to the maturity of the readers. Because the major purpose of graded passage assessment is to place students in graded materials, an attempt was made to create or to select and adapt materials similar to those in which the student might be placed. One set of materials (C) was developed for children in or near the grade-level designation of the passages; a second set (C/A) was developed for use with either children or adults; a third set (A) was developed for adults.

Questions were constructed to be as passage dependent as possible. Because recall is being tested as well as understanding, questions are literal. To avoid problems with passage dependency, inferential reasoning is tested apart from literal recall and is not counted in the total score. The *BADER Inventory* uses retelling as a way of assessing perception of organizational structure and as a less stressful, more efficient way of testing. McCormick (2003), Gillet and Temple (1990), and Alexander and Heathington (1988) recommend this procedure and cite the *BADER Inventory* as one of the few commercial tests using retelling.

An insufficient number of passages is read in graded reading passage testing to use categories such as vocabulary, organization, inference, and main idea in a reliable way (Schell & Hanna, 1981; Spache, 1981). Because of the insufficient number of passages read to provide an estimate of level of functioning, no attempt was made to differentiate significantly the passages by organizational structure. Most readers will have better recall of narrative passages than expository passages. Students' performance on both kinds of passages may be compared by selecting readings across C, C/A, and A sections of the inventory. Diagnosticians using this inventory reported that student interest in the passages was much greater than their interest in comparable test passages. Dr. Larry Kenney (1996), University of Wisconsin—Whitewater, asked students to read and compare passages from several published reading inventories and rank them as to interest and appeal. He reported that the Bader passages were ranked first, unanimously. Since interest strongly affects performance, this is the critical factor in more accurately estimating levels of functioning.

Readability was estimated with the Harris-Jacobson formula and the Fry formula. However, final adjustment of word selection and sentence length was made on overall content rather than on artificial manipulation.

Primarily to test the content, 30 elementary students, 20 secondary students, and 20 students in adult education read the passages. Passages that were not considered appealing were dropped.

Next, passages were tested for equivalence. Forty elementary students read C and C/A passages. Oral reading yielded a product-moment coefficient of .80, and silent reading yielded a correlation coefficient of .78. Forty secondary and adult students read C/A and A passages. The oral reading coefficient was .83, and the silent reading was .79. Fifteen older elementary students who were embarrassed by their poor reading ability were given the adult passages, in order to examine these passages' effect on attitude. Response was positive with regard to the students' liking the content of the passages. However, no statistical evaluation was attempted.

Dr. Daniel Pearce (1981), Texas A&M University, examined the validity of the graded passages as an instrument for determining reading level. Thirty students in grades 4 through 8 were administered the graded passages, and an instructional level was determined for every student. Next, each student's reading teacher was asked for the grade level for basal reader materials in which the student was receiving instruction. These teacher assessments were compared to the instructional level score obtained from the graded passages.

Bader and McIntyre (1986) compared the placements of 27 children, grades 1 through 5, with diverse ethnic and racial backgrounds from low-income families. University students were given a two-hour workshop on administering the graded word list and oral and silent reading passages. They estimated a reading level which was compared by Dr. McIntyre to the reading levels determined by the school reading specialist and confirmed by the classroom teachers. The correlation was .93.

The adult passages, word lists, and spelling tests have been used with well over 6,000 functionally illiterate adults from 1989 to 2003 by the Capital Area Literacy Coalition (CALC) in Lansing, Michigan, as well as other literacy groups nationwide, and have been found to be acceptable to the adult students and to provide reliable indications of their literacy functioning. Since 1990, over 6,000 children have been tested in CALC programs with high accuracy in comparison with school assessment. CALC was approved in 2003 by the Michigan Department of Education as a No Child Left Behind supplementary provider.

The director of Project READ, Redwood City, California, Kathy Endaya (1997), reported that more than 1,800 adults, youth, and children have been assessed with the *BADER Reading and Language Inventory* since 1989. To continuously check the accuracy of their results from administration of the Bader, Project READ compares their assessment composite with learning specialists' results at Sequoia High School, Menlo-Atherton High School, and Fair Oaks Elementary School. Endaya states, "The Bader assessment results have continued to be consistently within half a reading level of the schools' total composite of tests. Further verification of the composite comes from reading and learning specialists at the Foster City Reading and Learning Institute."

The National Institute for Literacy (NIFL) lists the *BADER Reading and Language Inventory* as an assessment instrument that is suitable for adults (http://www.nifl.gov/reading profiles).

Rate and Fluency

With regard to evaluating rate with comprehension, Richek et al. (2002) and Bond et al. (1994) agree that it appears to be hazardous to specify rates for different grade levels. Rate varies with the kind of material (controlled vocabulary, narrative expository), student background, and purpose for reading. Careful observation can reveal a lack of fluency. Whispering, pausing, rereading, and word-by-word reading are indications that the student is having difficulty with fluency and may be struggling with word recognition.

Examiners may obtain a rate-per-minute estimate by using a stopwatch to time the student's reading and dividing the time into the total number of words (exclusive of title) listed at the end of each passage. If the examiner's school district provides rate norms, these may be consulted. Most examiners would probably do better only to note extremely fast or slow reading, but the guidelines suggested as approximate by Rasinski and Padak (2000) may be useful:*

By second semester of grade:	1	2	3	4	5	6
Estimated words per minute:	80	90	110	140	160	180

Silent reading rate with comprehension should range from 200 to 250 words per minute for levels 7 through 12.

Although the definitions for *instructional level* and *independent learning level* are given in another section, further explanation is indicated for their use. For several years the writer attempted to follow the standard informal reading inventory (IRI) guidelines in much of the literature. Students were usually placed in materials that were found to be too easy. Although one can rationalize placement in easy materials for the legitimate purposes of building fluency and confidence, the placements were often not appropriate for direct instruction. Research on the problems of determination of instructional level through IRIs suggests the need for revision of the classic, stringent requirements of word-for-word accuracy and the need to weigh comprehension.

The general guidelines for reading levels are as follows: The *instructional level* is one where students comprehend at least 75% of what they read and can recall at least 60%. Students may be considered to be at a *frustration level* when they exhibit behavioral indications of stress, miss more than 10% of the words, and understand less than 60% of what they read. Students may be considered at an *independent level* when they miss no more than 5% of the words, read fluently, and comprehend at least 80% of what they read. Please consider these as general guidelines. The purposes of the graded passages are (1) to find the highest instructional level at which the student can comprehend and (2) to analyze reading to discover student strengths and problems in reading so that the student can be appropriately placed in materials for instruction. Little seems to be gained by *computing* frustration and independent levels.

Finally, one cannot ignore widespread classroom teaching practices. Many teachers place students in readers and auxiliary materials that require the student to do a great deal of independent work. Although one may question the value of some of these materials, students do use them and need to be placed in them about one level below their highest instructional level unless they are given direct instruction and support by their teacher. This is the *independent learning level.*

The inventory provides a window on the reading process "so that affective, perceptual, linguistic and cognitive aspects of reading can be observed" (Bader & Wiesendanger, 1989). It has potential for training prospective teachers about reading behavior, unequaled by other types of learning, and it allows a close match between testing and teaching.

*From *Effective Reading Strategies: Teaching Children Who Find Reading Difficult* by T. Rasinski and N. Padak, 2000, Upper Saddle River: Prentice Hall. Copyright © 2000. Reprinted with permission of Pearson Education, Inc.

OTHER INVENTORY SUBTESTS AND CHECKLISTS

Remaining parts of the battery should be selected and interpreted according to the need of the student to perform the task (i.e., complete mastery, or in terms of a comparison with peers). When research has suggested cutoff points, these have been recommended.

Emergent Literacy

Research reported by Morris et al. (2003) in *Reading Research Quarterly* provides a developmental sequence of early reading acquisition from kindergarten: (1) alphabet knowledge, (2) beginning consonant awareness, (3) concept of word in text, (4) spelling with beginning and ending consonants, (5) phoneme segmentation; and in first grade: (6) word recognition and (7) contextual reading ability. All of these abilities can be assessed with this inventory. Morris et al. emphasize the importance of "finger pointing," which is an evolving skill beginning in stage 3 and continuing to stage 5. *Word matching* and *syntax matching* are other terms used for this skill. In earlier research, the *syntax matching* term was used.

Carolyn Humphrey-Cummings (1982) administered the *BADER Inventory* Graded Paragraph test and Word List test to 123 kindergarten students to determine if they were readers or nonreaders. Next, those reading were classified as decoders, sight readers, context users, or combination readers by analyzing their performance during paragraph reading and their ability to complete the Semantic Cloze Sentences, read nonsense words from the Phonics Inventory, and read sight words. These groups were administered five of the inventory subtests that measured readiness abilities: naming letters, hearing letter names in words (beginning consonant awareness), syntax matching (now called word matching or finger pointing), writing letters, and spelling. All five of the subtests discriminated readers from nonreaders. Syntax matching was a significant task for all types of beginning readers. Syntax matching and spelling discriminated between readers using phonetic analysis and all other readers. Syntax matching and naming letters discriminated between sight readers and context readers.

Bader and Hildebrand (1992) extended research on emergent literacy by administering selected inventory tasks to children age 3 to 5 years to study prereading concept development. Generally, the emergence of observable, specific preliteracy behaviors did not occur until age 4. They concluded that variation in literacy, language, and symbol concepts is to be expected among 5- and 6-year-olds, dependent on their experience and rate of development.

Phonemic Awareness and Manipulation

Although phonemic discrimination and phonemic manipulation are not new areas of concern in beginning reading, they are getting a great deal of attention. Researchers, however, are not in agreement about which abilities predict success in reading. Yopp and Yopp (2000) provide sound suggestions for phonemic development. Most agree that phonemic awareness should be assessed by having students segment and blend phonemes (Richek et al., 2002). Segmenting and Blending tests are included in the *BADER Inventory* as well as tests of Rhyming and Initial Phoneme Recognition. In addition, information about these skills can be obtained by observing students' spelling and their ability on the Hearing Letter Names in Words test. Tompkins (2003) describes the letter-name strategy as an early stage in spelling development. There is evidence that phomemic awareness is acquired by some beginning readers as a consequence of learning to read (International Reading Association, 1998). When children have had instruction in beginning reading and continue to struggle, they may have difficulty in segmenting phonemes or in other language areas. If these problems cannot be overcome, they will need to be taught with approaches that do not depend on these skills or processes.

Open-Book Reading Test

The ability to read and respond to various texts can be probed more validly during trial teaching or classroom instruction than in the relatively brief time allotted for testing. The diagnostician is encouraged to construct open-book reading tasks (Bader, 1980; Manzo et al., 2004) or to use informal instructional sessions to assess abilities in academic or workplace areas for older children and adults. Guidelines for constructing open-book reading tasks are in this edition, but open-ended discussions that reflect the purposes of the reader are encouraged. The informal open-book inventory can be a valuable assessment tool for middle school and high school content areas and for workplace materials.

English Language Assessment

The English Language Learning Quick Start test and checklist have been used with over 3,000 refugees, immigrants, and migrant farm workers and their families served by the Capital Area Literacy Coalition. The Quick Start test provides a reliable guide to program and materials placement, as well as giving administrators, teachers, and tutors a way to communicate about and report levels of profiency. The checklist is arranged in a sequence frequently used by tutors and was validated by English language teachers and the Corporation for National Service Volunteers working with the coalition.

States have been developing their own English language assessments and curricula. Common categories for levels are beginning, intermediate low, intermediate high, advanced low, and advanced high. Teachers whose schools have their own instruments may want to use the Quick Start procedure when they need to wait for a formal assessment.

References and Suggested Readings

References in this section include early classic discussions of assessment issues as well as newer publications and inventory reviews.

Alexander, J. E., & Heathington, B. S. (1988). *Assessing and correcting classroom reading problems.* Glenville, IL: Scott, Foresman.

Bader, L. A. (1980). *Reading diagnosis and remediation in classroom and clinic.* New York: Macmillan Publishing Co.

Bader, L. A., & Hildebrand, V. (1992). An exploratory study of three to five year olds' responses on the Bader Reading and Language Inventory to determine developmental stages of emerging literacy. *Early Child Development and Care, 77,* 83–95.

Bader, L. A., & McIntyre, L. D. (Fall, 1986). Improving reading through university and public school cooperation. *Journal of Children and Youth, 7,* 38–45.

Bader, L. A., & Wiesendanger, K. (Fall, 1989). Realizing the potential of informal reading inventories. *Journal of Reading, 32(5),* 402–408.

Bond, G. L., Tinker, M. A., Wasson, B. B., & Wasson, J. B. (1994). *Reading difficulties.* Boston: Allyn & Bacon.

Cooter, R. B. (1990). *The teachers' guide to reading tests.* Scottsdale, AZ: Gorsuch Scaresborg Publishers.

Endaya, K. (1997). *Bader Reading and Language Inventory: Verification studies.* Unpublished manuscript, Project READ. Redwood City Public Library, Redwood City, CA.

Fahcy, K. B. (1996). Books/software reviews: Bader reading and language inventory. *ASHA Leader, 1*(4), 12.

Fitzgerald, J. (2001). Can minimally trained college student volunteers help young at-risk children read better? *Reading Research Quarterly, 36*(1), 28–46.

Gillet, J. W., & Temple, C. (1990). *Understanding reading problems: Assessment and instruction.* Glenview, IL: Scott Foresman/Little Brown Higher Education.

Goodman, K. S. (1969). Analysis of reading miscues: Applied psycholinguistics. *Reading Research Quarterly, 5,* 9–30.

Goodman, Y. M., Watson, D. J., & Burke, C. L. (1987). *Reading miscue inventory: Alternative procedures.* New York: Richard C. Owens.

Harris, A. J., & Sipay, E. R. (1990). *How to increase reading ability,* (9th ed). New York: Longman, Inc.

Hasbrouck, J. E., & Tindal, G. (Spring 1992). Curriculum-based oral reading fluency norms for students in grades 2 though 5. *Teaching Exceptional Children, 24*(3) 41–44.

Henderson, E. H., & Beers, J. W. (Eds.). (1980). *Developmental and cognitive aspects of learning to spell.* Newark, DE: International Reading Association.

Humphrey-Cummings, C. (1982). *Differences in the acquisition of selected readiness abilities between readers and nonreaders in kindergarten.* Ph. D. dissertation, Michigan State University.

International Reading Association. (1998). Phonemic awareness and the teaching of reading: A Position Statement from the Board of Directors of the International Reading Association. Newark, DE: Author.

Kenney, L. (1996). *A comparison of published reading inventories: Reader appeal.* Unpublished manuscript, University of Wisconsin—Whitewater.

Manzo, A. V., Manzo, U. C., & Albee, J. (2004). *Reading assessment for diagnostic-prescriptive teaching,* 2nd ed. Belmont, CA: Wadsworth/Thomson.

McCormick, S. (2003). *Instructing students who have literacy problems,* 4th ed. Upper Saddle River, NJ: Merrill/Prentice Hall.

Mercer, C. D., & Mercer, A. R. (2001). *Teaching students with learning problems,* 6th ed. Upper Saddle River, NJ: Merrill/Prentice Hall.

Morris, D., Bloodgood, J. W., Lomax, R. G., & Perney, J. (2003, September). Developmental steps in learning to read: A longitudinal study in kindergarten and first grade. *Reading Research Quarterly, 38*(3), 302–328.

Pearce, D. L. (1981). *Validity of Bader graded reading passages for determining instructional level.* Unpublished paper, Western Illinois University.

Pearce, D. L. (2002). A diagnostic inventory review. *The Reading Professor, 14*(2), 149–154.

Powell, W. R., & Dunkeld, C. G. (1971). Validity of the IRI reading levels. *Elementary English, 48*(6), 637–642.

Rasinski, T., & Padak, N. (2000). *Effective reading strategies: Teaching children who find reading difficult.* Upper Saddle River, NJ: Merrill/Prentice Hall.

Richek, M. A., Caldwell, J. S., Jennings, J. H., & Learner, J. W. (2002). *Reading problems: Assessment and teaching strategies,* 4th ed. Boston: Allyn & Bacon.

Richardson, J. (1994). Review: Bader Reading and Language Inventory. *The Reading Professor, 17*(1).

Rubin, D. (2002). *Diagnosis and Correction in Reading Instruction,* 4th ed. Boston: Allyn & Bacon.

Schell, L. M., & Hanna, G. S. (1981). Can informal reading inventories reveal strengths and weaknesses in comprehension subskills? *The Reading Teacher, 35,* 263–268.

Spache, G. D. (1981). *Diagnosing and correcting reading disabilities.* Boston: Allyn & Bacon.

Tompkins, G. E. (2003). *Literacy in the 21st century,* 3rd ed. Upper Saddle River, NJ: Merrill/Prentice Hall.

Yopp, H. K., & Yopp, R. H. (2002). Supporting phonemic awareness development in the classroom. *The Reading Teacher, 54*(2), 130–143.